From Stardom to Wisdom

Healing and Love Beyond the Spotlight
Vol. 1

Elandra Kirsten Meredith

Elandra Kirsten Meredith
elandra@healthhealing.org
www.healthhealing.org
www.kundaliniyogainternational.wordpress.com

Limits of Liability and Disclaimer of Warranty

Warning – Disclaimer

ISBN: 978-0-9892243-3-8

Published by Ant-El Productions
Auckland, NZ – Kapa'a, HI – Edmonds, WA

Praise for *From Stardom to Wisdom*

This is an amazing story of Elandra's transformation of her life with beautifully written and very insightful messages woven throughout. The book is a very fun read and Elandra's words and stories keeps pulling you along anxious to hear what happens next. The book is beneficial to all ages as it traces some very important and fun moments in the history of the 60's, 70's, and 80's to now. I highly recommend reading this book and feel everyone will be enriched by her many very positive messages in the story and words of wisdom that she shares.   *Rich Wonder*

Scenes from the Great Gatsby do not outshine Elandra's experience with all of the things the world can offer, but it is not enough. Readers who are familiar with current findings of scientists nominated for Nobel prizes for works in Quantum Physics will appreciate Elandra's experiences as she weaves a tale that moves through dimensions.   *Forever Learning*

In reading her autobiography, I can understand why Elandra is so dedicated to personal and planetary awakening and healing. Elandra's earlier life revealed the need to go deeper and release what was not real or lasting. In my view, Elandra opened up to the power of who she is as a mighty and love filled soul.   *M. M. Sophia*

This is the ultimate love story because it is a woman's journey in finding herself through yoga, spirituality and self-love. Elandra is an incredible storyteller and with her lifelong work studying consciousness and ancient wisdom, she brings the message of Aloha to us. This is a story of a celebrity-turned-yogi, wife, mother, healer, and seeker; an amazing woman who has had magical and life changing experiences.   *Lauren Orlina*

This is an amazing journey, an intriguing true story about one woman's coming to consciousness and beyond. It is a high privilege to read this book and to actually work with this smiling woman who, after healing overnight her shattered ankle, goes on to study, practice, teach and live her healing awareness of the body.   *Jo Ann Lordahl*

An inspirational story that will give you courage and give you a new perspective on what is possible.   *Katrama Brooks*

Elandra is a starburst of love and light! I read the entire book in one sitting, and felt cleansed and healed. Captivating, authentic, inspired and inspiring. Thank you more than I can say!   *Ganga Barret*

From Stardom to Wisdom" reads like a compelling novel but speaks with the authority of a holy scripture. Elandra's story makes the saying "truth can be stranger than fiction" come alive! It's a page turner that I highly recommend!   *Elizabeth Weber*

I really loved the book and her life experience, couldn't put it down for a full day and one hour! She is very authentic.   *Donna Diamond*

An inspiration for personal transformation... She has a flowing style that pulls you in... she is the love she teaches... thank you Elandra!
Angela Longo

This book is captivating indeed! What a challenge to carry out the message!
Earl Stokes

A dramatic autobiography, a spiritual journey, a true love story, a witness to the reality of at least one documented miracle. Plenty to ponder as to the range of human potentials - for good and evil - some damning observations of the uber-rich met in her early stardom. Plenty to wonder at here.
Wizard of Eutopia

I loved reading the book and gave me insight into the life of Elandra and her husband Antion. They are beautiful people full of love, life and laughter. Thank you Elandra for sharing your journey with us.
Manasi Gupta

I had the good fortune of meeting Elandra on Kauai, as a talented healer and immensely joyfilled lady! I enjoyed this book, one for not moving me through deep personal cleansing, but more of a light footed waltz through decisions and life changing events. Strung throughout are her pearls of wisdom.

Carolyn Thompson

It's always so refreshing to read someone who loves life and its mysteries, especially someone who will embrace all situations. I met Elandra and Antion at a community I was staying at and immediately knew there was heart and humanity in the work that they were doing which comes through in their yoga, music and conversation.There is a clear difference between them and the New Age army of the politically and spiritually correct. They show their human side.   *Tom Wanderer*

Dedication

Not only this book but my every breath is dedicated to my Creator and to my beloved closest family, who are all three born on the same day, Valentine's Day.

Antion Vikram Singh 'royal star of the lion', 'invincible warrior of truth', he is my Hero. His Hawaiian name is Pu'u Kani O Ka Lani, 'great sweet voiced singer of the heavens.'

Our two beautiful daughters, Pritam 'beloved of the Creator', and Siri Lakshmi, 'Great Goddess of wealth and abundance.'

All three are heroes and goddesses and my love for them is boundless and endless.

And to those whom I never forget: my ancestors, parents and relatives. My *Ohana*, wider family around the world, friends, visionaries, cultural creatives, sacred activists, evolutionaries, futurists, change agents, spiritual new agers, artists, musicians, singers, chanters, authors, peace-loving peoples and teachers of all times, as well as all the transformational communities whose lives are about being in service and envisioning, valuing and living Aloha Love, Healing and Truth for a better world.

Mahalo, thank you, I love you and thank you for being who you are.

Siri Lakshmi, Antion, Myself and Pritam, Seattle 2007

Preface

"The world will turn to Hawai'i as they search for world peace because Hawaii has the key…and that key is Aloha!" - Pilahi Paki, Hawaiian Kahuna

I love this quote. *Aloha* came to me as the answer to my fervent life-long hunger for a transcendent consciousness and wisdom.

Aloha has many levels of meaning; as a greeting it's similar to *Kia Ora* in New Zealand or *Namaste* in India, "my soul greets your soul." The syllables of the word make up the meaning "the joyful sharing of life energy in the present."

But it means so much more! It means the feeling of the presence of the Creator, and the divine beloved Creation, right here, right now…

And this *feeling* engenders a delicious state of loving acceptance towards all that allows no person or part (including oneself) to be left out. It is the feeling of being home, of being gifted with God, at the Source. It is Supreme Love, Divine Love, balanced Love, - beyond romantic, sentimental or attached Love.

The very word is a code. And a portal, a doorway to a dimension of living in a way that holds an authentic in-the-moment consciousness, - synonymous with happiness! And it's energy, a mindset, an 'attention', cognition, a consciousness, magical... yet totally present and practical.

And it's me! Aloha Love inspiring - and aspiring - to a world of global peace and joy - is my living breathing body, heart and soul's being.

Above all, Aloha – you can't define it! It's a very personal thing because it's a feeling, something you have to *feel for yourself, and define for yourself.*

So that's what I'm doing, sharing what it means to me, and encouraging you to do the same for you…what does the energy mean to *you, personally?* Aloha Love inspiring - and aspiring - to a world of global peace and joy - is my living breathing body, heart and soul's being.

This book is my way of sharing the Aloha by reaching out to you, and I would be delighted if you reach out to me:

Please visit my web site at www.healthhealing.org

Send me an email at elandra@healthhealing.org

Or write a review of this book at
http://www.amazon.com/dp/B00CAGLIN0

Aloha and Mahalo

Contents

Introduction

*Yesterday we obeyed kings and
bent our necks before emperors*

*But today we kneel only to truth,
follow only beauty*

And obey only love.

--Khalil Gibran

I'm known as a healer and a teacher.

I experience myself as a catalyst,

An awakener of your own body's ability to self-heal.

I'm a researcher, writer and promoter

Of the consciousness of miracle self-healing.

I act as a health and healing coach,

Consultant and catalyst for remembering

What is known somewhere deep inside you

And all humankind...

As a teacher of yoga, spirituality,

Women's work, health, and healing,

I love dancing - in all dimensions,

While sharing my wisdom about

"Living love" and "ageless living"

As fast as I can, at every chance I get.

This book is going to have to write itself,

With me surrendering to the process,

Because to perfect it would take too long,

And the thing is, it's time for it to show up now.

It was going to be a book on healing, miracle healing,

But suddenly it said, "Wait! We have to tell your story first."

My *kahea*, spiritual call and purpose, and *kuleana*, destiny and responsibility, is to share with you the insights garnered from my journey through the worlds of celebrity stardom, yoga and timeless Hawaiian shamanism. They encompass my 'initiations' during four decades of fulltime research, focused dedicated spiritual practice, over $200,000 worth of courses and classes, and practice of over 33 healing modalities internationally in five healing centers as founder/director of my own healing modality with international training.

My personal experiences, perceptions and perspectives come from my passion for finding the similarities and parallels in ancient timeless wisdom worldwide. Some of my understandings come from inner guidance and intuition, are unique to me, and may - or may not - be in alignment with information from known cultural history, organizations or authorities.

This passion and love has kept me seeking out teachers and wisdom keepers during many years of traversing the oceans from California or Hawaii to New Zealand. And if sometimes I sound as if I'm on a rant, that's why.

When as a healer I witnessed bones, cancer and cuts healed in front of my eyes and the almost dead coming back to life, I was asking, "Why isn't everyone seeing and recognizing this, why are our bodies and our world in this increasingly sick and perilous state, what is the consciousness and keys we are missing?" The answers started coming and my teachings and this book series are the result.

This first book *From Stardom to Wisdom Volume 1* is a bit of a mini-memoir serving as an introduction to my life's journey and work. Many of my most amazing stories, transitions and transformations will be included in my subsequent autobiography and healing books. In the interests of brevity, details such as dates, names, and locations have occasionally been changed.

My next book is focused on healing and transformational consciousness. My visions of a "new civilization" include some of my favorite writings from visionaries and sacred activists worldwide.

Some sections are called *"Elandra's Holo-Perception"*, short for *Holographic Perception*, which refers to a form of consciousness that holds within it 'bigger picture' simultaneity. It is explained in depth in Volume 2.

My third book coming is a 'how-to' book. How to live an authentic life of radiant health, inner and outer wealth; how to experience your own 'god-like' power to love, and to self-heal miraculously – and much more.

Although this first book of my series is not a how-to book, my loving intention is that my stories may:

• Inspire you to value above all your own intuition and inner truth

• Advance your on-going process of joyous transformation of consciousness for your own healing, fulfillment and happiness

• Provide support in your own "hero's journey"

• Implement your own insights for your soul's growth

So it is in this invoked spirit of Aloha, that I invite you to partake in - just a little - of my journey with me.

1

Born with a Vision

"The usual hero adventure begins with someone from whom something has been taken, or who feels there is something lacking in the normal experience available or permitted to the members of society. The person then takes off on a series of adventures beyond the ordinary, either to recover what has been lost or to discover some life-giving elixir. It's usually a cycle, a coming and a returning."

-- Joseph Campbell

One day you will awaken and you will know

That you know you are awake

You will know Love, because

Love is Who You Are,

Rather than what you do, have and give

You will feel Love in your cells

Because Love is your destiny

And Love is All There Is.

Love knows only Love

It is your touchstone,

Your yardstick,

Your Holy Grail,

Your Power.

I was born remembering there was something I had to re-member, and so was forever searching without knowing what for, searching the world, looking, longing...

And I found it – a consciousness, a certain kind. A consciousness that can create 'miracle' healing and one that I now know we can all access. It is the same consciousness that can transform our deeply troubled world to a heart-based world, and has even been predicted to do so within our lifetime.

I was born remembering there was something I had to re-member, and so was forever searching without knowing what for, searching the world, looking, longing...

And I found it – a consciousness, a certain kind. A consciousness that can create 'miracle' healing and one that I now know we can all access. It is the same consciousness that can transform our deeply troubled world to a heart-based world, and has even been predicted to do so within our lifetime.

This consciousness, which allows for the simultaneous accessing of numerous dimensions of reality, I have termed "Holographic Perception". Transmitting it is what my work and life is about, and telling my stories in numerous books.

In and with this consciousness, friends, even when I don't know you personally, I know you all the same. I know you are reading this. I know you, for whom I am writing.

2

"The Call" to Consciousness

*Denmark *Memory of Birth *Pioneers in New Zealand *Spiritual Search *University with no Wisdom *Intellectual Disillusionment *Return to Europe*

"Congratulations - you are among a select group of souls who won the lottery to be here, on this planet, at this time! The prize not only ensures you a front row seat but also the unique opportunity to co-create the future of the human race."

— Christine Page, MD

Elandra's Holo-Perception

From beginning to end, from birth to death, life has a start and a finish, and this progression creates a story. Life seen in hindsight and perspective is called the "hero's journey." Most stories - and good movies, such as "Star Wars" - are based upon what is called traditionally the "hero's journey." It's a bigger picture way of seeing life's journey as an archetypal progression: first into your ordinary world comes the call to awakening, to embark upon the adventure. You are scared; you resist. Then you get your mentor and you courageously set out to overcome the first threshold, the barriers and tests placed in your way. You get your allies, and then comes the "worthy opponent," the "supreme ordeal," the "Darth Vader" underworld challenges, the enemies. You conquer these monsters (that include inner discouragement, helplessness, and hopelessness, self-judgment and so on), thereby scaling the mountains and slaying the dragons. Victorious you return bearing the fruits - your surrender of ego and your resultant inner wisdom - to then claim the rewards, the resurrection, the princess or prince, the powers, the enlightenment, the freedom, the Elixir or Holy Grail.

My first picture

I arrived onto this planet with conscious memory.

I am here. Only about half an hour old, in the hospital alone in my crib noticing, thinking, aha! here I am, I made it here! Wow, there's bright blue sky through the window. Here I am, looking around this room resolving to remember my birth and what I am to do here on Planet Earth! I am seeing myself in this tiny body, and simultaneously everything outside this window, the whole city and country, and where I just came from! I have to remember this feeling!

It was wartime in occupied Denmark; the air imbued with inescapable unease. The country of my birth was taken over by Nazi troops. The sounds of their tramping, marching boots – as well as their shouting and shooting – resounded ominously in the streets of my little town of Odense.

Life was disrupted and food severely rationed. My brother and I lived with my mother's ever-present sense of danger and fear of violent intrusion. We never knew when the Nazis would show up at the door, demanding food, bicycles, and who knows what else, at gunpoint. My father coolly faced them. He had dismantled the bicycles and hidden the parts under the floorboards.

Mostly we stayed indoors. My mother's hands were never idle; she sat sewing and knitting all our clothes, making something wonderful out of nothing, with amazing talent, artistry and mastery.

One time the Germans deliberately murdered someone as a premeditated show of force to intimidate and terrify the populace, especially the underground freedom-fighters. For maximum shock value they chose a person of high standing, a doctor. They hauled this innocent doctor out of the nearby hospital and shot him right there in the town square, in full view of the stunned populace.

We were out one day when we came across shooting in the streets; full of fear I ran as fast as my little legs could carry me.

My older brother and I had few toys and little to occupy us, so I would watch him lie on the floor under *Mor's* desk chair (Danish for mum, mother), playfully patting her thighs and legs. Although I was less than two years old I remember this because, just at that moment came the dreaded knock on the door. We knew we had to immediately hush up and take our places, hiding under my mother's long skirt.

At night Mor – Karna Andreassen, neé Rasmussen - would read to us from Hans Christian Anderson, the famous writer of fairy tales who was born close to where we lived. The reading was from the original Old Danish, old fashioned and unfamiliar to her, not watered down by translation into modern Danish.

I loved the mysterious, deep dark and incomprehensible, the more strange and impossible the fantasy the better! She didn't like it though, she would interrupt her reading with frustrated interjections, protesting, this is just so weird!

I was enthralled by the atmosphere that imbued these tales, the juxtaposition of the real, down to earth, tragic and horrible in life with the sense of heroic transformational magic, that anything and everything is possible.

At two years - 1945

My body responded with sensations that made me feel so alive. I loved the chills, goose bumps and shivers. I felt I was connecting with the whole of humankind, the universal collective-consciousness of humankind, with all its pain, depth and tragedy.

Perhaps it could be healed by feeling, loved and healed in the reading, even unconsciously, even by a little two year old, even by me. I fantasied that I might live my life like him, creating comforting worlds of fantasy, while having to live in a harsh reality.

To help pass the time Mor would draw tiny figures on paper and I would watch with bated breath as they came to creative life, with this or that dress or coat or hat on. She always drew them as father, mother and two children, boy and girl. Sometimes they were bears: invariably the mother figure wore an apron, and father was always depicted in overalls and great big work boots.

Those little bits of paper represented a whole world to me and I cut them out carefully and reverently, gave them names and characters and a life with purpose and marched them round the tiny apartment. In my imagination they were alive and real, talking and listening to each other and to me. They were my companions.

My Parents on their Wedding Day

My father – Poul Lindhom Andreassen - was hardly ever home, he worked very hard all day and then went to another job as a night watchman. *Far* (Danish for Dad) was only 25 but was already suffering from arthritis because of working in extreme cold as a welder. But he had a dream that kept him going.

One rare day he drew a picture for us kids. I watched eagerly as he began sketching blue sky, a beach with waves, and palm trees. I stared enthralled as he drew another tree and then added bananas growing on it. (I had never seen or tasted a banana but that made it even more exciting.) My mouth broke into a big smile as he drew a bright yellow sun into the blue sky, and then he put us into the picture, standing there smiling big, all of us, our whole family, standing on the beach with magnificent smiles. Finally he added two hula girls, their grass skirts swaying in the breeze.

Watching him draw this picture made me feel thrilled in my belly, like having butterflies in there, and happy in my heart and warm in my body. Something very special had happened, something that would live in my heart forever, and as our glowing hearts warmed up our little apartment in cold miserable wartime Denmark a seed was sown in mine...

During those years of deprivation and fear my father was working towards his dream, saving every penny towards the huge cost of getting his family to a place of safety, freedom, warmth and peace, far away from war-torn freezing Denmark.

At four years - 1947

The longed for day came, the news of freedom! Denmark erupted in exultation! The Nazis were withdrawing and the Danes went wild with rejoicing. The streets were ours again. My four year old brother cleverly escaped the house through the gate, and took off on his tiny bicycle, in search of adventure, boldly exploring the town while his frantic family searched for him. It took all day for the police to find him and return him home, and he was beaming, radiant with satisfaction when he finally fell asleep that night.

My mother had learned in early childhood that when things were bad, there was nothing you could do, "You have to put up with it." So she was good at the stiff upper lip, repressing her feelings and rarely showing painful emotion. When she was telling me the story that upon arrival at the border the Nazi troops were forced to abandon their loot, she was actually crying. Her emotion was so strong, I wondered if they had stolen something from her personally or her family, something she could never talk about.

In the weekends we would go by bicycle to visit the countryside where my parents' families lived, in Orbaek and Skellerup. I loved the farm smells, the haystacks, the attic full of apples, the cows being milked, and the cherries getting picked.

Far kept working towards his goal, determined to find a better life, somewhere in the world with a warmer climate. Since he had a sister already living there, New Zealand became his choice. My family prepared to set sail for the far ends of the earth, not knowing if we would ever see our country, family and friends again.

Leaving Denmark 1950

The day came when my beloved *Bedstemor* (grandma) took me out to the garden and said, "Listen to the birds singing farewell to you, hear the earth, trees and vegetables saying goodbye."… My little heart was bursting with feeling as I sobbed, "Good bye garden, good bye all you beautiful birds and flowers and shrubs and trees, and vegetables, I love you and I will miss you! Good bye little bench I love to sit on! *Have det godt!*" (be well)

Our pictures were in the newspapers when we left Odense, Denmark.

I was six, my brother John was eight, and Lars, four. All our relatives cried. We embarked from Southampton England for the six week voyage. We knew no English, and my mother was in tears at least once every day which confused me, because after all this was a great big fun adventure for us kids! After six long weeks with strange English food that we didn't much like, strange language and kind but even stranger people, we docked in Wellington, and then travelled by train to Auckland, initially to stay with Dad's sister.

There we found her and her five children being abused by her violent husband; he actually tortured the cat in front of us for his own amusement. We were all in shock but knowing not a soul, nor the language, we were trapped with nowhere to go and no money.

Far learned English as fast as he could while looking for work by bicycle and bus. His plan was to build a tiny house, move into it, then buy a small piece of land and transport the house there. He did – within a few months - and it stands there to this day. He would then build us a big beautiful home… which he did within a few short years. That too still stands, as do our other beautiful homes and gardens in NZ.

Many years later we heard that my cousins left home as soon as they could, and seeking to escape all memory of their father, deliberately destroyed every single picture and record of him from their lives. I never saw them again.

These early times were very challenging; we had no refrigerator, no radio, no phone, car, washing machine, no music player, no TV, few toys and books until much later.

School was terrifying. Abandoned on the school playground the first day at school, I kept my eyes fixed on the one and only familiar thing I knew: my older brother. My body felt completely tense inside for fear of losing sight of him; he was my lifeline.

Because I didn't speak English, how could I even ask to go to the potty, and where was it? While writing this I came into a memory that in my helplessness I had wet my pants, a traumatic, humiliating event I had repressed.

One day I was reading aloud to the teacher. Because I stumbled over an unfamiliar word she hit me, forcefully slapping my hand with a ruler. I turned a deep red, flushing with humiliation and shame, feeling betrayed and sick inside my body. I didn't need punishment to motivate me to learn! I loved learning! Why didn't she know that?!

When I was a baby I would think, "How strange, the people here talk to me like I'm an ignorant baby knowing nothing." Feeling this way remained with me, even when I was in school I kept thinking, "How weird this school thing is. I already know everything, yet I have to act like I don't and pretend to learn it all over".

One time we were given an essay topic which threw me into a state of grief-stricken, inconsolable sobbing. Inside me was some frightful loss. My heart was breaking, in sheer anguish and, unable to identify it, I simply could not stop wailing. I cried uncontrollably for hours, to the great concern of the teacher who had to call for help from the principal to take me out of the class room.

The topic was simply "Write about a shopping trip with an Aunt". But I had no Aunt to take me shopping! I had no family! Although my Mor had seven sisters – to say nothing of my Far who had ten siblings – they were eleven thousand miles away! I missed them terribly, the people who loved me, my aunts, uncles and cousins, my grandmothers and grandfathers! And I missed *hjem*, (Danish for home) our home in Denmark. The teacher, principal and classmates were sympathetic.

As best we could we stayed in touch with them, at a time when there was no phone or planes, and letters took 6 -8 weeks by sea to reach us. Every single letter and package from hjem was eagerly and excitedly welcomed. One Aunt, *Moster* Inga was like an angel to us; she most often sent presents, all of which we valued and treasured beyond belief. As time passed we formed community with other Danish immigrants who became as family to us, sharing and helping each other. They became my surrogate aunts, uncles and cousins and this helped to fill a void.

Still I was deeply lonely for something. I would go exploring alone down to the river near our house and imagine my long lost love, my knight-in-shining armor, who would come galloping up on his stead, seize me by the waist in his strong arms and haul me up behind him, and we would ride away to our true home in joyous glorious reunion.

I always had a crush on someone, some secret beloved sweetheart, one of the boys at school. I loved the sensation of love in my heart as I longingly fantasized finding soul communion with him in some deep magical divine intimate understanding. Of course they never knew.

In spite of my initial traumatic experiences, it was surprisingly easy for me to learn English. My neighbor lent me some Donald Duck comics, and seeing the text issuing from the mouth of the characters, along with the drawings of the action, all I had to do was guess what they were saying. It made total sense, so learning the language was a breeze, and soon I was top of the class in all subjects, a position I maintained for the whole of my school life. Sometimes I scored so high that my marks brought the class average way up. It was so easy I couldn't regard it as any accomplishment.

From age six and onwards there was a feeling that never left me: wonderment at the whole system of formal teaching and learning. To me it made no sense. Why did I have to learn all over again what I already knew? I couldn't understand why it was not the same for everybody. I kept looking for answers and in the absence of books in my classroom, reading whole encyclopedias before I was 10 years old.

I was beginning to realize that my body's feelings were my best feedback, a way to calibrate the truth. My body would give me signs I could feel and understand so as a child I watched for signs everywhere. My feelings of joy at being in the beauty of nature, the love in my heart recognizing the power of art... my body knew my vision and I was learning to trust it to lead me forward into the unknown. The way my heart would leap up and my body shiver was my clue...

With so few toys and books, imagination was my life. I created a secret game; I would pick up lost handkerchiefs, (no tissues in those days) in the playground or street, take them home and surreptitiously lovingly and reverently wash and iron and fold them. Some were pretty flower designs, delicately embroidered, some plain plaids - I carefully gave them names and characters just as I had with the paper dolls as a tiny child. I imagined them as my friends, my long sought after soul playmates, of deep understanding and wisdom and love. I played endless games with them, laying them out and moving them around to hug and share and talk to each other. They were my people.

During these years of growing up I never doubted being wanted and loved by my parents, and felt blessed to be part of a family where love was expressed through creative cooking, baking, sewing, house building, green thumb gardening, nurturing and beautifying house, home and everything. We had several beautiful fish ponds and my parents planted many fruit trees, cacti and flowers. My father created his own home welding business, and mother helped. I felt fortunate and proud that my parents were so enterprising, highly motivated and not into alcohol and smoking.

Out of necessity the New Zealand Kiwi culture of those early days was very do-it-yourself. When I was eight my parents made me a pram; Dad had acquired the wheels somewhere, and welded the body, and Mum sewed the lining of the inside of the collapsible hood as well as the bedding and beautiful doll's clothes. (I still have it and intend to get this homemade creation into an early immigrant museum in Auckland or the Danish house). Then with the same DIY proud spirit my parents designed and built us a big beautiful house, and it was tremendously fun and exciting to move in even before all the floorboards were down.

Our Boat

Several joyful memories stand out in what I felt was a privileged upbringing. Near my home a small library opened up within a store, and it was with great excitement that I would hurry in there on my way home from school searching for more of my favorite adventure books about seafaring. So one of the most exciting days of my life was the day that we got a boat, there it was being towed into our driveway! It was a 40 foot slender hull that needed work. Watching my father and brothers excitedly designing and building the cabin was so much fun, and when it was finished, wow! We had a grand launch with lots of our Danish family and a big party that lasted all night.

The Danes knew how to have great parties, they loved their *smørrebrød* (similar to the Swedish *smörgåsbord*) with *Akvavit* (strong Danish spirits) and Dad would dance nonstop all night with every single lady there. Then - to my amazement because I couldn't keep my eyes open any longer - they would all take off on our boat to watch the sun rise. We loved our cruises to some of the many beautiful islands out of Auckland.

On Our Boat

Dad rarely sang, but on these occasions he would often be happily singing "Oh what a beautiful morning, oh what a beautiful day". It was deeply exciting to make landfall at some unknown uncharted little deserted island where I would have the feeling of being the first human being ever to set foot there, what an adventure being a pioneer was.

I was always searching for my place, how I could fit in, what was important to me. One day I heard the word 'psychology', and got this feeling of excitement in my body. Ah, this must be what I am looking for, even though I had no idea what it was. It must be something to do with feeling and consciousness and senses and the unknown, and my direction and destiny. Maybe psychology was about the feelings, about the senses. I wanted to learn about this.

One of my Ballroom Dance Outfits

At high school I was an all-rounder, prefect, vice-captain of hockey team, straight A student and a ballroom dancer with the highest marks ever given in NZ. In my last year of high school I started modeling for TV commercials. In the late 50s in provincial NZ women – both young and old – were expected to dress properly and act elegantly. Although we were only teenagers we wore formal corsets, gloves, and carefully coiffed hair.

Do the right thing, like get married by 23 before you become a spinster forever, (the good men will be gone) get a house and have babies and live a normal life. That was what our community of elders expected of us girls.

As a high-achieving student of exceptional promise and honors, I believed I could find the truth and wisdom that I sought at Auckland University, where I had been accepted on a Teacher Training scholarship. Once there though, I felt lost and lonely; I had no one to whom I could express my feelings. I started acting in plays – from which I found great enjoyment – but I could not escape the feeling there was no place in this world for me and my consciousness. I had no real friends and felt alienated. I enrolled in

Psychology and what a disappointment, oh so impersonal, intellectual, pedantic, controlling, uninspired and boring, oh my, I hated it!

Disillusionment set in. I began to identify with the great authors and poets whose works I was studying in my literature classes. I could understand that, by taking their own lives, they were removing themselves from a world where they had no peers. I had no one in whom I could confide - no such thing as counseling in those days – and so I contemplated joining those suicidal, literary giants, all the time carefully hiding my loneliness and depression behind a ready smile.

To me, their lives, who they were, were way more important than the literature they left behind. I wanted to talk to them, save them, love them, heal them. To answer silly questions about them in a stupid exam seemed like an insult of the highest order. Every month I would spend some days contemplating how best to commit suicide. Much later I came to realize how these times coincided with premenstrual syndrome, a word unknown in those days.

I finally discovered a book that spoke to my desire for spirituality. It came like a refreshing drink of cool water in the desert of my longing. The book was *Autobiography of a Yogi* by Paramahansa Yogananda. It fell open at his picture and I fell in love, reading voraciously about his search for direct experience of the Divine Mother. My unhappy soul found a home in this book; it exuded the connection, intimacy, wisdom, and spirituality for which I longed.

The folk band *Peter Paul and Mary* came to town, and seeing Mary's long straight natural hair, lit a fire in me. I wanted what it symbolized - freedom! Self-sovereignty! No matter what my parents wanted for me, and no matter how much I felt I owed them, I was here on this planet for a reason, and a future of a sweet life in suburbia was not it. Now New Zealand seemed small, provincial and confining. I wanted to explore my roots in the old world, Europe; I had to get back to my original home.

I dreaded the idea of a "normal" life stuck in a nice, new suburban house. This wasn't my idea of a meaningful or worthwhile life. I was on a mission for something bigger than me, whatever it was. Although I could by no means be called worldly-wise at that young age, I was aware that something was going wrong with so-called Western Civilization. Even back then, fifty years ago, I felt that people were being conned by the society of which they were a part!

After winning World Formation Team Competition

Mum especially wanted me to live a "normal" life. She was a stay-at-home mum who was a wonderful cook and housekeeper, how perfect for us kids! So in spite of my feelings, I still felt an obligation to "do right" by my parents. Mum worried what I would do when I grew up, fearing and projecting that I would be as helpless in the world and in need of a husband as she had been. In her whole life, her relationship with Dad was her one and only relationship. For Mor, daughters had to get married.

One day while walking the university grounds a strange thing happened. Inside my head I was hearing a tune and when I identified it, I was horrified: it was the silly song "Here comes the Bride". I took it as sign that I had to follow the destiny society had laid out for me. It was while acting at university that I had met a young British professor of Latin and Greek. Somehow I knew we would marry before he proposed. Maybe this was the special relationship I had been seeking; it seemed as though my future was settled. I didn't know how I was supposed to feel, yet I was aware that the feeling of being in love that I treasured as a child was… nowhere to be found. I was just trying to do the right thing.

So, partly for tradition's sake – but mostly for my parent's sake – we had a big fancy wedding doing all the right things. I wanted to believe in these traditions, and be a good daughter. Mum sewed my elegant, exquisite wedding dress as well as those of the four bridesmaids. I was a professional model at that point and looked beautiful in it, as did the bridesmaids in their gorgeous dresses. We all went to the hairdressers, got fancy hairdos, and then had a lot of beautiful studio pictures taken, because that was what you were meant to do. It was the tradition, wasn't it, so you had to do it. Mum put on an elegant, Danish smorgasbord; a sit down feast in our home for a hundred guests, and did all the cooking herself. Dad made a wonderful speech.

Mum designed and sewed my wedding dress 1965

Shortly after the wedding my new husband flew off to England to take a position at the University of Bristol. I would follow by ship, taking six weeks to reach the UK and stopping at such exotic places as Tahiti and Acapulco. But I wasn't interested in stopping at any port of call, because I had all my favorite books with me, and looked forward to staying in my cabin and having uninterrupted contemplation time.

After all, an exciting life in academia awaited me and having studied art and languages at one of the world's best universities, I liked to think of myself as an intellectual, a serious minded student and a researcher of consciousness in this phenomenon called life. Little did I know that this voyage would change my plans and my personality so totally that I did not even touch my books, and caused me to arrive in England a completely different person.

My mother was losing her little doll, her sweet model child, her only daughter, her exceptionally both brainy and beautiful daughter. Just as my parents had left their families, both my older brother and I left NZ for Europe, never to return to live – at least, so far.

England was pure culture shock, I felt horribly out of place. I missed the barefoot casualness of Polynesian New Zealand which had instilled in me an easygoing worldview. My sudden exposure to the rigidity of English attitudes and class-consciousness was unbearably stultifying. I had hoped that living in the hallowed halls of academia would bring some satisfaction to my ever searching soul, but I was sadly disappointed. All I found was dry intellectuality punctuated with cynical one-upmanship.

I didn't know what to do. I applied and was accepted for a position as a high school teacher of German. Simultaneously someone had recommended me for a job helping organize entertainment at Britain's largest, most exclusive country club and, rationalizing that I could always return to teaching at a later date if I so chose, I decided to accept the offer.

My university experience as an actress, model and ballroom dancer stood me in good stead as I found myself ideally suited for the job. This would assuage my boredom, and my need to be connecting with people. The club booked many of the world's best entertainers and I loved chatting with famous musicians, singers and performers, such as Harry Belafonte. Some propositioned me while showing me pictures of their wives and children; as if doing that would make them more attractive? I hated men hitting on me, yet also never wanted anyone to feel rejected or hurt.

I would take breaks in the tearoom with all the employees of the club, including the kitchen staff, and was amazed to discover that class distinctions were very important to them. If they considered themselves lower class, they were proud of it, and that was that. They had a station in life which was home to them, they would never dream of trying to better themselves, it just wasn't done.

I also realized that it's your accent that mostly determines your place in the rigid British social class structure. My New Zealand speech placed me outside the standard pecking order and gave me a certain freedom as they were puzzled about how to pigeon-hole me.

One day I accepted an invitation to visit London and went by train, alone.

Landing in London, stepping out of the Underground for the first time, I'm awestruck! The very air is vibrating with an explosive creativity, and I'm shocked and enthralled to my core. There's room for me here! This is what I've been looking for forever, something bigger than me. I am blown away with the sense of potential and possibility, the excitement of a big city, the culture, the arts, ballet and architecture - everything I'm longing for must be here!

London at the time was a hub for global culture and an exhilarating place to be. This was the wild swinging London of the 60s - California flower power, Kings Road, Carnaby Street, famous designers like Ossie Clark, the mini skirt, hot pants, burn-your-bra, and 'free love' times. As an innocent from provincial New Zealand, a skinny 21-year-old used to wearing very conservative formal corsets, careful skirt length, and gloves and matching purse - I was excited and I was hooked.

It wasn't long before I found myself living in the midst of all this excitement. At first, I would visit my husband on the weekend, then once a month. Finally it became obvious that we were separating. He was a kind and understanding man. As my new life claimed me we accepted our parting with mutual respect and goodwill.

I was crossing Park Lane where I lived one day, and in the middle of the road I heard a voice addressing me, "Excuse me." I turned and there was a man staring at me. Before I could respond he said, "You ought to be a movie star." I said "Okay!" and he became my agent.

3

Actress in London: Getting "Killed" - Again

*Movie Star Career *Burnt at the Stake
*Killed for Being a Woman and a Healer
Jimi Hendrix and his Death

Elandra's Holo-Perception

In ancient times storytelling was the very essence of life's cultural organization. Learning took place through direct experience of life in nature along with the oral traditions handed down for aeons for particular purposes. As Clarissa Pinkola Estes says, "A story is not just a story... it's someone's life, and the firsthand familiarity makes the story 'medicine,' a medicine which strengthens and arights the individual and community."

As I stand there trembling in silent, sullen terror, they tie my hands onto the crossbar of the stake. My eyes search frantically for a friendly face among the crowd that has gathered - someone who would speak up for me, beg for mercy on my behalf. There are none. Their faces are hard, impassive; no one dares to speak up for a woman accused of witchcraft. Eyes glinting with fanatic righteousness and vengefulness, the ringleaders light the branches piled around my feet. As the flames lick higher I begin to scream and writhe, trying to break free. I scream myself hoarse as the flames reach above my head.

"Cut!" yelled the director. The hard-boiled film crew broke into spontaneous applause, an unheard of compliment in the tough world of British film making.

Burned at the Stake in *Twins of Evil*

This was the final part of the Karnstein trilogy, *Twins of Evil* (1971), made by the legendary doyens of British horror movies, Hammer Films. I was playing an innocent young girl wrongfully accused of being a witch, hunted down by religious fanatics and burnt alive. For my immolation, Hammer had created a set with meticulous attention to detail. I was tied to a stake and surrounded with brush that would be set ablaze at a signal from the director. There was real fire all around me, and even though I had been heavily sprayed with fire retardant, a nervous medical crew stood by in case of accident.

On the day I heard, "You ought to be a movie star" that corny line provided an immediate entrée to a world hitherto beyond any girl's wildest fantasies. My "Okay!" led to a blur of being photographed, creating a portfolio, being interviewed, and attending auditions as the "Yes's" piled up from casting directors. I appeared in the Peter Sellers movie *The Magic Christian* (1968) and found myself working alongside other luminaries such as Ringo Starr, Roman Polanski and many more. I was also cast in an all-star version of *Julius Caesar* (1969), with Charlton Heston, John Gielgud, Jason Robards, Richard Chamberlain and Diana Rigg.

In 1970, I landed a role in *Crescendo* with James Olson and Stefanie Powers, the first movie that I did for Hammer Films, the famous British horror studio. It was through them that I acquired the cult fame that persists even now 40 years later.

That same year I appeared in five episodes of the highly successful London Weekend Television comedy series, *Doctor in the House*, playing the girlfriend of one of the young medical students. The gig involved performing on stage for a theatre audience while being simultaneously broadcast live on TV for 50 million viewers - so no retakes, let alone "rushes." It was new, challenging and exhilarating.

Towards the end of that year, I filmed the role for which I will forever be remembered by a legion of Hammer Horror aficionados: the stunningly beautiful "First Vampire" in *The Vampire Lovers*.

As the movie opens, a vampire hunter, Baron Joachim von Hartog played by veteran Brit actor Douglas Wilmer, stands on the battlements of a ruined castle on a misty moonlit night. The Baron, in voice over, relates his desire to avenge the cold blooded murder of his sister. He watches as a hooded spectre rises from a grave a short distance away. As the apparition leaves the graveyard, it drops its shroud. The Baron descends from his vantage point to pick it up, reminding the audience that a vampire will always return to retrieve its shroud.

After gorging on the blood of a young man in a nearby village, the creature returns and is clearly perturbed not to be able to find its shroud. The Baron taunts the creature by waving the shroud from the battlements of the castle. Seeing this, the vampire heads towards the castle as the Baron mentally prepares for the confrontation he has precipitated.

As the hunter stands waiting for his prey, resolute in his intention yet clearly scared out of his wits, the scene cuts to a shot of a beautiful young girl in a translucent white gown. The Baron is transfixed by her bewitching beauty and, in spite of his resolve, his fear and his desire for revenge, he is unable to move. In front of him is the vision of a lovely woman. Her face, her loving eyes, her lips parted in a kind smile promise all he has ever dreamed of in a woman. She moves towards him in offering invitation, floating ethereally, gracefully, hypnotically and rhythmically, one step at a time ascending the dramatic backdrop of the ghostly staircase.

He awaits her, paralyzed with anticipation, fascination and excitement. Her focused consciousness is charged with the power of implacable intent. Step by step, dramatic tension rising, She is closing in on her prey, She must have him and nothing will stop her from fulfilling her desire. Tension builds as the fatal confrontation nears. She is ready to open her mouth and position her vampire fangs to sink into his neck; ready for the moment of ultimate vampire ecstasy, the death embrace.

The moment is here! As her mouth opens for the fatal bite and her barely covered breasts press against his chest, the camera zooms in sharply. The crucifix at his throat burns her and she recoils, wide eyed with horror.

That brief millisecond is all that's needed to bring the Baron to his senses. Suddenly remembering the sword still clutched in his hand, he cuts off her head. Blood spurts graphically as her head rolls away down the stairs.

The credits roll: Hammer Films presents: *The Vampire Lovers.*

That shot of me gliding seductively toward the Baron is one of the most iconic of the Hammer images. I'm bemused to find, all these years later, that photographs of this scene still turn up for sale on e-bay.

Happily, it was not my own head that was severed. Hammer had previously commissioned a life size plaster replica to be made. It was that effigy which was decapitated in the movie. It took them two days to build the mold around me as my whole body had to be encased in plaster. When it came time to cover my head I had to fight to stay calm.

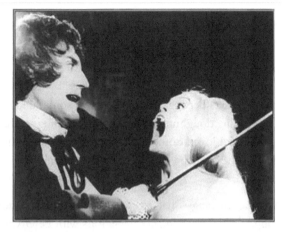

The Baron (Douglas Wilmer) about to cut off my head

This must be what it's like to be helplessly buried alive. I felt very vulnerable to think my life depended on sucking in a bit of oxygen through two straws sticking out of my nostrils! I was paralyzed, unable to move and barely able to breathe. What if someone knocked out these straws accidentally or there were an earthquake or fire at that moment? I would be done for. I had to stay in this claustrophobic situation for an hour.

Once again, Hammer outdid themselves. The plaster dummy was a perfect likeness with beautiful blonde hair, eyes, eyelashes, eyebrows exactly like mine (my arched eyebrows had always been darker than my natural blonde hair) and all! The artistry was superb.

For the beheading shot, they had first to prepare the neck of the plaster replica for the sword stroke. A local butcher provided a few fresh steaks to match my neck size. A balloon was filled with fake blood with fake arteries sticking out, and placed inside the neck. Then the meat was stuffed into the throat, and the arteries threaded through from the attached bag of blood. Thus when sliced through with the sword the blood could spurt out in an impressively authentic manner, with perfect coordination and artistry! I have always been amazed that they would spend so much time, energy and money on what the movie audience would see for a mere split second.

I loved making these movies. I loved the drama of the Gothic castle darkness and the spooky stairs. I loved the cobwebs that were shot out of guns. The Hammer technicians were such perfectionists. They prided themselves on getting every detail taken care of in the most aesthetically pleasing manner. I particularly loved meeting and interacting with the other actors and actresses.

I was proud of my vampire fangs; they were so perfectly made, necessitating several trips across London to be fitted by Christopher Lee's dentist. On the set breaks between shots there was something delightfully challenging about eating doughnuts with these protruding teeth, it was almost impossible and I loved doing the impossible. It wasn't just the taking of a bite, but the chewing and then the swallowing…no problem for real vampires.

While I was wearing my fangs I had to speak with a lisp; that didn't stop me from having long, deeply satisfying conversations with Peter Cushing who appeared in *The Vampire Lovers* and *Twins of Evil.*

Peter Cushing

Peter Cushing, of numerous Hammer movies, (and currently an active Facebook Appreciation Page) was endlessly graceful and charming. He was a wonderful listener, and I found a sympathetic ear for my life story and my soul searching.

"What was it like leaving Denmark at the age of six to arrive in a foreign country and not to be able to speak the language?" he asked me. "Did you like New Zealand? I've heard it's so beautiful!"

I told him of my interest in yoga to stay healthy but most of all to gain in awareness.

"That's right, Kirsten", he said. "I became an advocate for vegetarianism for the same reasons."

Talking with Peter was like relaxing in a large spacious room with ample air to breathe, I felt like I could talk to him about things which I could never hope to discuss with almost anyone else in my life.

At the time, I was also performing with a traveling masked theater company, playing Chekhov and Shakespeare. The founder director was from Greece where they have an ancient tradition of theater using masks. I was having strange experiences wearing these masks and felt that such an experienced actor as Peter Cushing could give me some insight.

Publicity shot for the *Masked Theater Company*

"Peter", I said one day, "When I'm behind the mask I feel myself becoming somebody else, an archetype as ancient as the world itself. It's like…goose bumps stuff that just happens spontaneously, a strange voice speaks out of my mouth; a voice that seems to know things, to have actually existed before. This is not acting as far as I know! But I am fascinated. What do you think?"

"Yes, something that you didn't learn about and hear about can be scary." He replied. "But that makes for mind opening growth and depth. In Greece they understood these things; that's why their ancient theatre was so powerful. In our culture it is different; you come initially from a place of separation, rather than spontaneously from within. When you can let go of what you know, think you know, and just be open, waiting, a force takes over and you become creation itself. And you are one with it, and in that oneness there is great joy and excitement for both the spectator and yourself."

As he spoke, I felt his encouragement and acknowledgement. It was quite gratifying. Yet I realized there was more, something I was sorely missing; it was wisdom. The kind of wisdom for which I had been searching in vain throughout my years being just another university intellectual. Many years later I would develop a way to consistently harness and wield wisdom in another field.

Glamor shoot for *The Vampire Lovers* 1970

Hammer Films organized a photo shoot with all the Hammer Glamor actresses in the movie: Ingrid Pitt, Kate O'Mara, Pippa Steele and Madeline Smith. The five of us were photographed in the same gowns that we wore in our scenes. My diaphanous vampire nightgown was not fitted, it was loose and transparent, and I worried that it was inclined to fall down a little too far accidentally and end up revealing my nipples and all in full view. Everybody else had nicely fitted gowns for the publicity stills, and I had no other clothes but this non- fitting non–garment! I suppose they made this gown that way on purpose, it had to be a one size fits all. A vampire fashion to titillate as well as to suggest certain timelessness. Later I found someone to blame: a man named Todd Browning, who directed *London after Midnight*, an early horror movie from 1927 that starred Lon Chaney, was the originator of the tradition of female vampires wearing loose, diaphanous negligees.

By now my pictures and interviews were showing up in the international press as well, in newspapers and magazines in my native Denmark, in New Zealand, and even in Pakistan.

In 1971, I appeared in the second movie of the Karnstein trilogy, entitled *Lust for a Vampire*. Again I met my demise before the credits rolled, this time as an innocent peasant girl whose throat was slit and whose blood was poured over the rotting remains of a semi-deceased vampire to bring her back to life.

Despite being "killed" numerous times in grisly ways, my career was on an upswing. After an appearance in the BBC comedy series, *Birds on a Wing*, at the end of 1971 I was signed to play in the TV series *The Persuaders*, a program centering on two playboy sleuths. The producers had secured a sensational coup in casting two larger-than-life figures in the lead roles: Tony Curtis and Roger Moore. For my own part, I was no newbie who was going to meet an early and bloody end but a co-star. This was my best role yet. That I was suddenly a leading lady working shoulder to shoulder with some of the biggest stars in the world caused the press to call me the upcoming Marilyn Monroe or the next Catherine Deneuve.

Roger Moore, Me, Tony Curtis - from a Danish magazine

Making movies demands an early morning start, usually at a studio some distance from Central London. I often had to force myself out of bed at 4am with my usual late night dance-club-smoke and alcohol-induced headache and drag myself to the studio via taxi. For the shooting of *The Persuaders*, however, a chauffeur-driven shiny limousine would be sitting at my doorstep. There was a bar in this limousine with a rose in a vase. There were international newspapers and all kinds of liquor to choose from. Did I pour myself a gin and tonic to start out my day at 4.30am? No, instead I wondered... about why this was considered desirable and luxurious in this world.

I was excited that I would soon meet my almost unbearably handsome and debonair co-star Roger Moore. It wasn't just his looks - the make-up crew spoke of him with near adulation, telling me he was unfailingly good natured, even at 6:00am, throughout the seven years of filming the TV series, *The Saint*, the program that had made his fame. Amazingly, he had even greater charisma off-screen than on. His twinkling eyes, sparkling humor and attentiveness created a magnetism that was unreal. We hit if off together - as he must have done with all his co-stars.

My fame was increasing exponentially. A fan magazine ranked me "the 11th most charismatically beautiful woman in the world" ahead of Ursula Andress, Raquel Welch, Farah Fawcett and many others. Supposedly, there were at that time 40,000 actors out of work in London, so I knew my successful career was due to my Scandinavian blonde looks and sex goddess image, but I was still baffled by it. I loved beauty in art and architecture, but had never understood the craze for beauty in a woman, and actually could not see that I had any! I valued intellect much more than beauty. And although I was not yet aware of it, I valued spirituality most of all.

Roger Moore and Kirsten Lindholm.

Dazzling Kirsten

BOB MONKHOUSE and his " Golden Shot " team certainly seem to like Danish girls and Yutte Stensgaard has started something by making such a hit in it.

Yutte, so much in demand in other TV shows, has left the programme. So they have

looked around for another Danish beauty and haven't had to look far, either. Kirsten Lindholm has taken over.

Viewers are seeing more and more of this dazzling blonde who has been featured as the hostess-type in the TV thriller in the House ", and numerous other shows, plus commercials for such items as cigars and Portuguese wines.

And when the Tony Curtis-Roger Moore series comes to the air Kirsten will be one of the first of Ois leading ladies to be seen with them.

Keep your eyes on her, Kirsten is going places!

Press clipping from April 1971

Soon I found myself on the inside of the London scene. Every night I was either at another swanky party with the cream of London society or I was dancing in one of the top discothèques. Previously, I had lived what felt like a dichotomy; one part of me a serious and introspective scholar, the other an extrovert, getting off on being watched wildly dancing the night away. Now the scholarly side began to sink from view as I took up residence in swanky Mayfair, partied and danced wildly till dawn.

Although I was becoming acquainted with many of the richest and most famous people in the world, I didn't much like most of what I saw in this milieu. On one occasion, I was taken on a tour of an exclusive home owned by one of the richest men in the world. The location was mind-boggling.

 In fact you may think I am making this up. You might even refuse to believe it. But it happens that telling the truth is always more important to me than anything else, certainly ultimately more fun too. So you see, I lived right there in the center of London in a very exclusive area called Mayfair. Nearby, well, we all assume, don't we, that beneath the ground of a gigantic city would be massive infrastructure, with all the plumbing and electrical wiring required for a vast city. (I just read that London has 46,000 miles of sewer pipes!)

Our assumptions being assumptions are not always the truth. There was something else – underground dwellings, maybe cities. Admittedly I don't know how I got there, I think I was riding in this enormous elevator descending somewhere, and then - I stepped out into a huge subterranean magnificent mansion! I still see the scene clearly! The centerpiece of this lustrous, rich man's splendid underground playground was a huge pool, built from glass, surrounded with gorgeous vegetation, statues and art pieces.

Would you believe it, it was a city of self-indulgence beneath the ground in London. Was it was filled with exotic fish? No, it was filled with beautiful, naked, large-breasted women, swimming around for somebody's gawking entertainment. I don't believe they had closed circuit television in those days. They may have had of course, - there are so many things we don't know or are deceived about as I was finding out, in my innocence. I was shocked.

There were many appalling experiences that were coming my way, but the experience that most shook me to the core was finding myself in the house of Jimi Hendrix right after he died. I assumed an ambulance had just taken his body away, because his girlfriend, Monika Danneman, was so wildly distraught she was on her feet pacing back and forth and round and round, madly chain-smoking with shaking hands. The room was thick with smoke, fear and horror.

It made no sense to me. How could it be that this beautiful man, this epoch-changing wondrous musician, legend and spirit of the freedom-loving sixties, was dead?

And how could it be that he had endured a ghastly end choking on his own vomit? No, no no! It could not be true. All this forcefully brought to my realization that the hedonism I was flirting with had a terrible downside.

And why was I there? Why was all this being shown me? There must be a reason.

You haven't yet opened your heart fully, to life, to each moment. The peaceful warrior's way is not about invulnerability, but absolute vulnerability - to the world, to life, and to the Presence you felt... a warrior's life is not about imagined perfection or victory; it is about love. Love is a warrior's sword; wherever it cuts, it gives life, not death.

--Dan Millman, The Way of the Peaceful Warrior

With Roger Moore

DANSK EKSPORT

Hun er dansk, hun er dej-
lig, siger englænderne om
den 25-årige Kirsten Lindholm. Kirsten har netop
sikret sig med i London,
hvor hun har flæt foden
indenfor ved TV-selska-
berne, som har givet hen-
de et par småroller. Hun

er født i Danmark, men
som ganske lille kom hun
til New Zealand, hvor hun
hurtigt fandt ud af, at hun
ville være skuespillerinde.
Det er så endt ved at lyk-
ken for hende nu, hvor
englænderne har fået øje
for den kønne pige.

4

Movie Star Meets Rock Star

*Disillusionment with Fame and Fortune *My Yoga Destiny *The Night My Life Changed Forever *Divine Illumination*

"Those who do not understand when enough is enough,

can never have enough!"

--Lao Tzu, Tao Te Ching

"The crisis facing humanity today is, at its root, a crisis of consciousness.
We are being called to put into practice the perennial wisdom of the ages."

--Peter Russell

Elandra's Holo-Perception

Under these circumstances and with this freely sharing intention such stories act as energy
transmitters. They are transmissions having the ability to move energy, to trigger change
(which is what evolution is) - sometimes instant change and healing in self and others.
When shared with pure intent, authentic honed experience brings about "group
consciousness". This activates in turn a healing "medicine" for the benefit of all.

In the spring of 1971 I met some American spiritual seekers who had been to see Sri Aurobindo and the Mother in Pondicherry, India. I was wary of cults and gurus, mainly because I had heard that some were just after people's money. When these Americans told me about a yoga class in Notting Hill, West London which asked for contributions but left the sum to the discretion of the student, I decided to try it out.

I showed up there straight from a modeling assignment and felt out of place in my very short "hot pants" and full makeup; if it hadn't been for the friends accompanying me, I would have turned tail. In those days any exercise was in the form of sports. There were very few public gyms and no such thing as aerobics, so this was way radical. I had never seen anything like it. At the front of the room up on a dais sat this man with a turban and a long beard, dressed in white clothes, t-shirt and jeans.

My yoga teacher - Vikram Singh - from Yoga and Health Magazine 1971

He was demonstrating what we had to do, while frequently yelling "Keep up!" I was shown a spot on the floor and found myself surrounded with sweating, half naked men and women in long white dresses. They were all copying the teacher precisely. Their breathing sounded like locomotive trains going "choo choo." I was in shock - it was another world, a totally freaky scene.

When the time came to lie down and rest at the end of class, my body shook and vibrated with energy. I was exhilarated. It felt great! So in spite of my initial trepidation I was drawn back and became a regular participant in the classes.

After a few classes, I began experiencing incredible inner sensations. I would see visions of yogis meditating in caves on the snowy slopes of the Himalayas. I recalled that, when I first read Yogananda's book as a teenager, I had felt something similar.

Over time I became more and more involved with the yoga students at the ashram. They were interesting to me, especially the American adventurers who found their way to the UK branch of what was an essentially American yoga group. They were in the forefront of the consciousness movement, and already knew a lot about healthy living, food and diet, massage and ecological living.

Yoga class 1971

Their expansive and open attitudes were very attractive to me. Talking with them, connecting with their consciousness was like opening a wonderful new space in my heart. Something speaking to me saying, "Hey, come over here, there's more breathing room!" Their effusive disposition seemed to reflect the vast geography of their country, as well as the pioneer, adventuring spirit of the early immigrants who found their way to this far distant country in search of freedom.

My yoga teacher, Vikram Singh, (Antion's name at the time) was also an American, even though he had been born and brought up near London. His father had been American and the few short years that he had spent in California had only served to confirm his American – and especially Californian – attitudes towards life.

He had been part of the world of privilege in which I now lived, and had walked away from it. Known in the music business as Vic Briggs, he had been a rock star, lead guitarist with *Eric Burdon & the Animals*.

One day it occurred to me that I hadn't seen the teacher's girlfriend for quite a while. I ventured to ask, "What happened to Debbie, I haven't seen her for a while?" He answered, "Well, she reluctantly followed me into this new lifestyle as a yoga teacher, but it turned out that she liked me a whole lot better when I was famous rock star and lived the Topanga Canyon yuppie lifestyle. She never really wanted be part of it, and actually the Yogi warned me she "wouldn't last". Well, she didn't; she's gone."

Eric Burdon and The Animals 1967 - **Vic Briggs far right**

Then he asked, "What happened to the guy you used to bring to class sometimes?" I pointed to the other side of the room, "Over there!" "Really?!" He exclaimed in surprise, "I didn't recognize him, he looks a lot thinner?" "Yes, I split up with him, that's why, but we are trying to be friends still."

I felt sad about him, my American former-boyfriend, who still occasionally would show up for class. I mused, why are my relationships never lasting? I had to let him go because on some level I wanted… more commitment. I wanted him to step up to the plate, though I didn't even know what that meant to me. It was my second breaking up experience and I didn't like it, I hated to hurt anyone. He was an American, an artist, an innovative designer and I learned from him about vegetarianism and macrobiotics. But I was looking for more.

At this point I was in yet another relationship, my third relationship since leaving my University professor husband. This latest boyfriend was from Australia. He had rugged good looks and an adventurous, bold attitude towards life. We had recently traveled through danger together, scaling the highest mountain in Europe, and then sailing from the Mediterranean up through the canals of France and across the dangerous waters of the Bay of Biscay back to England.

But could I trust him? In spite of this success at adventure, on an intimate level he seemed self-absorbed; I couldn't respect him, and so certainly couldn't give my heart to him. I could not bear the thought of being betrayed, to have my lover and husband - the love of my life, to whom I had given my loyalty and my life – one day suddenly cheating on me. In "Swinging London" I saw this happening all around me. And so I decided to not trust anyone, be free and uncommitted, even as another part of me longed for eternal commitment.

Vic Briggs 1967

There was a part of me, contrary to my conscious intentions, that wanted to be swept off my feet by someone very strong and focused who had purpose in life and willingness to truly commit to me. All the men I had met so far were the kind who would leave their relationships at the drop of a hat for another woman, - hey, I often felt that as I entered a room, they would abandon their wife for me, just for my looks! Yuck, did I hate that feeling! If being dropped for another could happen to them if could happen to me too! I started to despise this weakness in men, and wondered about this thing called beauty that would catalyze such craziness in them.

It was Christmas at the Ashram and all the students were gathered for dinner. Some items were needed to complete the dinner that was being cooked. I unexpectedly found myself alone with my yoga teacher - for the very first time, - as we were heading for a nearby Pakistani grocery to pick them up. As we walked along the road he surprised me by speaking personally about himself, saying "I'm looking for a good woman". I said nothing, felt nervous that he was confessing something so personal, just out of the blue speaking intimately, and… what did this mean to me? Why was he saying this to me?

Suddenly shaky and giddy inside, I put on a sophisticated worldly-wise air and began to talk to hide my confusion and vulnerability. I found myself telling him about the problems I was having with my latest boyfriend.

Soon after that he astonished me by inviting me to go out for the first time. Of all things, he wanted me to go with him to meet his mother, even though he wasn't in the habit of going to visit her on a regular basis. I had never been invited on a date to meet someone's mother before. We set out from the ashram in his VW van. I tried to cover my unease by making small talk the whole time there, not knowing how to behave in this unfamiliar situation.

Coming home I was even more jittery inside. I needed to break the tension, regain a sense of control over my life, and release some pent-up energy. So when we reached the Knightsbridge intersection, at about 10pm, in my typical spontaneous way I suddenly suggested, "Let's drive through the park!" "Why?" he asked, with some skepticism in his voice. "I want to hug a tree".

As soon as my feet hit the ground I felt better and laughing and giggling I took off at a run towards the nearest tree I could throw my arms around. I loved nature, and instinctively knew it would help me feel more grounded and more myself.

In that moment I didn't care what he thought, I had to have an outlet for the energy, my exuberant enthusiasm taking over. It came naturally to me to be spontaneous to release or move some energy. It was part of my nature even from an early age to believe there was magic afoot.

I knew he was looking at me askance with his best British reserve, thinking, is this woman sane or what, why is she doing this? No one had ever head of hugging a tree in those days. And of course nobody in Britain had heard of "sustainable" anything, and there were neither treehuggers dot com nor any eco green buzzwords.

One night I was at yet another party. I call this "The Night My Life Changed Forever." Everybody who was anybody was there – probably many of those celebrities I have named already - and that's just how it was at these parties. Julie Christie, Michael Caine, Ursula Andress, even Margot Fonteyn and Rudolf Nureyev were among those in attendance. That night I talked to some of the royals, Princess Margaret and Lord Snowdon, one of the glamour couples of the era.

Hot pants - in fashion in 1971

Even the presence of the Princess and her husband couldn't disguise, for me, that this was just one more star-studded celebrity party featuring an endless procession of behavior that was becoming more and more distasteful to me as I was becoming more and more sensitive to it. Jockeying for prominence, fawning, stripteases, excessive imbibing of drugs and drink, food throwing and conversation consisting of shallow one-upmanship small talk, always pushing for more, bigger, better - what was the point of all this?

That night, something happened inside me. I couldn't pretend any longer. Wealth and power and what it did to people suddenly seemed to me utterly unattractive. It was neither enchanting nor glamorous but on the contrary, useless, worthless, revolting, and even obscene. Hand in hand with that realization, came the recognition that the power I had via my beauty was worthless. I had long since realized with a sense of shock and even horror that I could walk into a room and feel that almost every male there would be willing to leave his partner at the drop of a hat if he thought he had any chance with me. I came to hate this feeling and this kind of power. This was neither who I was nor what I wanted in life.

What I was seeing over and over confirmed to me that celebrity society was built around the lust for more, more and bigger and better everything, fame, status, money and power; power over others - the power to be more and have more than the person next to you. With this mindset, enough was never enough.

Many of those outrageously rich and arrogant jetsetter types already had way more of everything than they could possibly ever use. Yet that didn't stop them - men and women both, but especially the men – from having a look of undisguised, unquenchable avarice in their eyes. Their life was about getting and taking as much as they could, regardless of the consequences to others. Their lives were a testimony to legitimizing and glorifying their limitless greed.

I had started to feel a certain hardness and non-caring within myself, which was very disturbing. I was afraid the company I was keeping was rubbing off on me. My integrity, my truth-seeking had always been my pride and joy, of paramount importance to me. It was slipping away; that which I valued most was in great danger of disappearing altogether.

I didn't know the word 'psychopath' in those days, but the predatory look of these people who were used to getting whatever they wanted was becoming all too familiar. I knew I had to try to make some sense out it. What I saw was that too much power and too much money corrupts those who possess it - in a way that is unimaginable if you have not seen it... up close.

Portrait - 1971

My experience and observation was that many of these rich and famous people looked down on, even despised, those who were not equally addictively ambitious, lustful and greedy. To them people were there, not just to be used, but to be abused. In their ever growing addiction to power and money they had come to believe it was an admirable virtue to not care about people.

I wish I were not writing this but I have to. Their entertainment was to find ways to subtly or openly further trample on others with a mindset of "snuff 'em out, useless ants", – and chillingly, all for entertainment. I hold back from saying more.

Vikram Singh had been a friend of Jimi Hendrix and one of Jimi's favorite guitar players.

I thought about the quote attributed to Hendrix, "When the power of love is greater than the love of power, there will be peace on this earth." I wondered if Jimi had brought about his own death, leaving his fame and adulation because he couldn't stand the world's greed for power.

I wondered, can everything and everyone in this world be bought? Does everybody have a price? Will all humanity sell their soul for power, status, ownership, money, sex or beauty? Will humanity be able to choose "power of love over love of power?" Will I? I asked myself, "What kind of power am I wielding? Is this the kind of power I want? How do I find a way out from a society immersed in this addictive, insatiable, toxic hunger for more power?" I had no answer.

Then a thought came to me: somewhere in this universe there had to be something else. What was going on, who was I and why was I part of this scene? Why had I been present at Hendrix's death site so soon after his death? Why had I been shown the repugnant, degenerate and debauched side of this kind of existence? I felt an enormous pressure building in my heart. Somewhere within all these questions was an answer. Something had to happen, something had to give, and something had to shift. I knew that I had to take a stand. I had to do something.

The intensity of my feeling was such that it manifested what happened next. As if a prayer were being answered, energy surged up in my body and took me over. Some inner force was propelling me to leave the luxurious couch, from which I was observing the proceedings, and was magnetizing me toward my coat and the door.

I stepped outside alone. My breath clouded in front of me. It was about 2:00am and cold, very cold. Aware of the inherent great danger of being a woman walking alone in the middle of the night on the streets of London, I started to cover my face and my long blonde hair with the hood of my white fur coat, but suddenly I let it drop. It didn't matter; I didn't care. I decided that tonight I would survive any danger. There was a force within me that nothing could deny and nothing would stop.

In my conviction of purpose I felt huge, powerful, and invincible. My stride was intensely resolute. Rising up in me like a raging torrent was this certitude: there had to be something better. There had to exist somewhere, something, to give me an authentic reason for being alive. There must be someone who cannot be bought or sold or compromised. There had to be in this world somebody living with pure intent - somebody with honor, and commitment to truth, goodness, and nobility. I would find that, because nothing else will do. Nothing else matters. That's it.

I realized that I was being drawn as if by a magnet towards an apartment in Notting Hill. I banged on the door. Despite the fact that it was now probably about 3:00am, the door opened and Vikram Singh invited me in to his yoga center studio as if he had been expecting me.

The picture on the wall of a meditating saint with a halo around his head greeted me. It represented Guru Nanak, a saint, mystic, musician, singer chanter and healer from the India of 500 years ago. His eyes seemed to be twinkling at me. Under the picture, a caption read, "Truth is High, but Higher Still is Truthful Living."

Vikram continued his meditation sitting cross legged. I sat facing him, about five feet away. He began to recite out loud what I later learned is a poem of praise of the Creator – Guru Nanak's Morning Prayer, known as Japji Sahib. I was watching him when an extraordinary thing happened. Around his head appeared a halo, but not a small one like you see in paintings, or like the one that used to appear above Simon Templar, Roger's character in *The Saint*.

This was a big expanse of light, a field of light! It was a huge encircling unearthly brilliant deep blue light that extended some four to six feet out around his head. It was an indescribable radiance, a field of deep color, a scintillating translucent shimmering brilliance of blueness...

In wonder and shock I was taking this in when something else showed up. Superimposed over this divine blueness now becoming background were thousands of sparkling, flashing golden streaks! Oh wow! They were blinking gloriously, magically, magnificently, while I just stared, open mouthed, awestruck, thrilled to my depths, in wonder - and in bliss.

I have no memory of how I got home.

In the ensuing weeks my life assumed a frightening intensity. I was stunned and moved by my recent experiences and also determined to ensure that the lessons I was learning did not slip away from me. What was happening, why had I been shown such an extraordinary sight? The sheer power of it all scared me.

My fervor for yoga only increased over the Yuletide period when my fellow yoga students engaged in seva, selfless service, also known as karma yoga. They had all gone to clean the bathrooms at a shelter for down-and-outs on Christmas Day. I was impressed by this focus, this selfless egoless devotion to service.

In the London Ashram 1972

I was becoming ever more mentally obsessed with this whole thing. I loved the yoga, and the committed, disciplined vibration and atmosphere I had never known before. The devotional music Vikram played and sang at the end of class put me into an altered state, an ecstatic place inside.

At the same time I was feeling more and more concerned about my attraction to all this. I started to worry, was I in love with him? I didn't know. I'd never had this feeling before, nor ever been in love before, not like this. It was new. I wished I had someone to talk to about it. I was afraid that I might be falling in love with him and my concerns were tearing me apart.

5

Past Lives, Persecution and How Power Corrupts

Richest Man in the World Drowns in his Soup
*Remembering Previous Lives *Witch Hunts
History

"We shall require a substantially new manner of thinking if humanity is to survive."

--Albert Einstein

And, for an instant, she stared directly into those [...] eyes and knew, with an instinctive mammalian certainty, that the exceedingly rich were no longer even remotely human."

--William Gibson, Count Zero

Elandra's Holo-Perception

One of the purposes of telling your stories to an audience, - whether in cyberspace out there, somewhere, or in a group setting and circle, - is as in ancient cultures, to empower you to remember that you too are part of history, living a story. We all have a story. By having a story to tell, and bringing it forth, you too can feel that you are more than your story. You can feel that you are in charge of your life, health and healing. You can feel then, that life is about cultivating your own joy and love for a better world in co-creation with others. But more, you might be remembering little by little ... Who You Really Are.

The day when I was to be filmed getting burnt at the stake I had no idea how very much I would be affected by the scene personally, and what it would bring up within me.

In these movies, getting cast as a victim to be sacrificed, my head chopped off with a sword, or ritualistically slit at the throat, seemed to be a developing pattern in my early actress days, with variations, like being blasted open at the heart with a shotgun, dragged off a galloping horse or done in by a vampire. It wasn't until much later I starting realizing that all experiences, even role playing, are a reflection of what you need to bring to consciousness.

I was beginning to reflect on what all this was about. Was something trying to tell me something? Was there something here I needed to become aware of? I started to realize that on some level, energy wise, I was being 'killed' or 'killing' myself constantly in my everyday life! Because it happened over and over in my real life that I couldn't speak out what was on my mind when I was afraid, angry, or needed something, or wanted to say no to the continuous propositioning from men. I felt paralyzed, nothing would come out, or it would be a strangled sounding croak.

However I was becoming practiced at expressing through screaming, even becoming known as "the screamer!" When the camera crew was dropping their cameras to applaud, everybody in the vicinity were experiencing some big hair-raising, some major 'goose bumps'.

No wonder, for strangely, the 'performance' they were applauding felt all too real to me. I screamed like you wouldn't believe. I screamed till I brought forth much of my own true fear about the circumstances I found myself in. I sounded terrified because I was. Later when I learned about past lives it made more sense. It was like I was reliving not just one but several previous lifetimes on that day - lifetimes during which I had suffered dramatic deaths by immolation for the satisfaction of thousands of spectators. For what? I got it: for the crime of being both a female and a healer.

The reason it was so intense was that we were enacting a scene that had actually happened in reality, in history, to hundreds of thousands of women. My research indicates that this took place during the time period of 1460 to 1670. The Inquisition was the organization created by the Pope for the express purpose of hunting down and killing women, wise women. The patriarchal Roman Catholic Church was intent on gaining more power and control. Anyone who did not go along with this agenda was believed to be a threat and those believed to be a threat were to be hunted down and put to death publically by hanging, torture, boiled in oil, strangled or burnt at the stake, along with anyone suspected of defending them. The Church had tens of thousands of women murdered, some say millions, and one source said 3 million. The last witch hunts took place in England in 1684, in Germany in 1775, and in America 1692.

The church wrote popular witch hunting manuals such as The Malleus Maleficarum which proclaimed women's intuitive powers were "of the devil," and use of herbs was "a cover" for witchcraft. Good deeds were suspect; healing itself a nefarious act. The worst sin was to alleviate suffering - whether through childbirth or illness - because suffering and dying was a necessary punishment for sinners.

And it gets worse, unbelievably one authority states: "By witches we understand not only those which kill and torment, but all diviners, charmers, wizards, commonly called wise women and men, and especially all good witches, which do not hurt but do good, which do not spoil and destroy, but save and deliver, especially them! It would be a thousand times better for the land if all of them be put to death." These manuals were published in eight editions and many translations.

So doing good was punishable by torture and death. Anyone showing compassion and kindness were suspect. Wow. This may explain a lot too, about the feminine values not being much valued in our world including by women. Yes, no wonder I screamed.

What's interesting is that according to some sources the persecution of women started long before Christianity. Before that about 6,000 years ago there was a time period that lasted around 4,000 years where throughout Europe, according to the findings from 3,000 sites and 30,000 sculptures, there was an agrarian egalitarian stable and advanced society. It was centered on the feminine values of the Great Goddess, family, community life, love of beauty and passion for justice, commitment to love and cultivation of wisdom and deep respect for Mother Earth. The Goddess was synonymous with Nature Herself as it is in Hawaii even today. There was no hierarchical system in which men were subjugated or suppressed. This was the Neolithic time between 7500BC and 3500BC. One source, an archaeologist for 30 years in Crete, Nicholas Platon writes, "In those times the fear of death was almost obliterated by the ubiquitous joy of living."

Wow, doesn't this sound so heart-warming! Is it true? In Crete, maybe, in Europe, some say no, no real proof. I would wish it to be true both then - and now!

So what happened? My source says that around the 5th millennium BC armed invaders swept down and destroyed these peaceful societies. They had a vengeful male god, glorified war, and invested in technologies of destruction and domination. They sought ever more power and were threatened by the feminine spirit of women and especially women healers. Over the centuries they deliberately defiled everything feminine including the nurturing spirit of women, until the entire female sex was looked upon as inherently depraved, a deceiving temptress.

Reading about this, I thought, why did this happen, who were they, and then what happened? So one source says "Science came along to be deified and the devil became an anachronism. Man's energies were redirected from torturing and enslaving women to the grander more important task of torturing and enslaving Nature Herself". Francis Bacon proposed that the domination and control of nature be the goal of the new scientific method, to "torture nature's secrets from her." He wrote that "Nature, like women, should be hounded, subdued, constrained and 'bound into service'." So Nature and the female were tormented and defiled first in the name of God and then in the service of science.

Explains a lot? No wonder I screamed. Reflecting on this persecution in our ancestry I think also of the fact that throughout history there have been peace-loving nonviolent societies, such as the Cathars in France and the Waitaha of New Zealand. They both ended up being slaughtered as they stood, not defending themselves. Their dead bodies were desecrated. Are we affected by this now? And how are we affected?

Was this then my call, a call to recognition and to self-healing? This persecution lives on in our bodies, organs, cells, genes and DNA. It lives on in there, in our bodies, until we resolve to re-member, recognize, and heal it by bringing it to consciousness.

I was being made to remember...this is the task up for me, - and I believe for the whole of humanity, - to solve, in order to evolve, by the task of remembering more, of who we really are.

So in this life's story, there in 1970, I was having ever more powerful spiritual experiences in the yoga classes. Something was happening to me that I did not understand. And more and more I found myself wondering about my lifestyle. I began to question my entire life. Yes, it was all glamour on the outside, but where was it - that something I was still seeking and not finding? It seemed I was no nearer to it than I had been while studying at University.

I was about to witness my next eye opening experience. I was right on track to being brought face to face with my ever evolving awareness of destiny calling. Around the time of being flown to the south of France to audition with director Broccoli for a James Bond movie, I went to Switzerland to film a commercial. During this time I was to be shown another jaw-dropping experience that deepened my growing disillusionment with the company I was keeping.

This was Gstaad, the exclusive playground of the rich and famous. I went with a party of jetsetter socialites to what I had been told was the most expensive restaurant in the world. It was New Year's Eve and the richest man in the world (again, according to what I had been told - maybe some ruling Prince from the Orient someone suggested I should marry), sat opposite, flirting with me.

Suddenly he was collapsing, falling forward over the table, face-first, right into his soup bowl! It looked like he was drowning in his soup, and nobody was taking any notice! I was in shock, not knowing what was happening; oh my, was he on drugs or having a heart attack?

Somehow what was horrifying me even more than his predicament was the lack of concern of the people sitting at the table. Nobody even paused in their gossip! Eventually and very casually, - were they used to this? - somebody removed him, took him away. And then he was gone. As if he had never been!

It was New Year's Eve, and no one cared about him one little bit. Nor did they care about each other. They were all too intent on showing off, trying to come off better than everyone else.

Seeing more and more such incidences I found myself secretly wondering, suspecting, and then deciding that hedonism and impoverishment of soul must go hand in hand. And as for me, what was happening inside me? I again had cause to wonder about my own integrity, and whether I was losing it by hanging out with people like these, super-rich with zero moral values nor even basic humanity?

I returned to my life in London thinking, no more glitterati paparazzi life for me! I had seen too much, that was it! I had to find a different kind of riches, a different power than that which money and beauty could buy. I had to find something, somebody who could not be bought.

"After I heard the lion roar "You have no idea how strong my love is!!! I came out of that meditation cave like a warrior queen."

--Elizabeth Gilbert, Eat, Pray, Love

6

Ram Dass Advises Go For It!

*Ram Dass Guides Me to Spiritual Commitment *End of London Acting Career *Spiritual Destiny Calls*

"Warriors of consciousness have an ulterior purpose for their acts, which has nothing to do with personal gain. The average person acts only if there is the chance for profit. Warriors act not for profit, but for the spirit."

--Carlos Castaneda

"There is only one journey ... and that is going inside yourself."

- Rainer Maria Rilke

Elandra's Holo-Perception

In the old days and in the old ways when we had no written language as such, or books or computers, learning would take place around the fire, sharing stories. We call this in Hawaii "talk story." It's a participatory sharing format where the story teller (or the elders in the circle) welcome questions and input from all the listeners. It is understood that the co-creative intention and spirit of the gathering and the wisdom derived from this openhearted sharing is for the freely given good of the whole community, and that we are all in community and communion with all things, even right now, all the time...all for the purpose of remembering... Who We Really Are.

Just when I needed it, direction came in the form of a famous author and holy man. Baba Ram Dass (former Harvard professor Richard Alpert) arrived in town on a stopover from India on his way back to the USA. His book *Be Here Now* was the most highly valued and well-quoted textbook of enlightenment of the times and next to the Bible, the biggest selling book ever.

Perfect! I had already been invited to meet him at Heathrow Airport with some new American friends. There were just the three of us, and I felt good about that as I would have plenty of time with him and he was travelling alone. I resolved to speak to him as soon as possible about my dilemma and fears.

As I spotted him walking towards us, I noticed something very unusual; this was no ordinary man, no ordinary occasion. There was this energy in him and around him coming from, I surmised, his mindboggling experiences in India - his surrender to and love of his guru there. His aura was huge, shimmering and vibrating with India, holiness and spirituality. Suddenly an amazing thing happened; his face disappeared to my sight, just vanished in a blinding great light.

Next his whole body was gone, as if he had turned into pure light. Nothing could be seen but this light - brilliant iridescent, irradiating pure light, white golden light that seemed as intensely dazzling as the sun itself. It was lighting up the whole airport even on this dark grey day with no sun in the sky! I was shocked, beyond awestruck.

Ram Dass with his Guru, Neem Karoli Baba

A few days later I made lunch for him at my Woods Mews, Mayfair apartment. Alone together I took the first opportunity to spill out my problems, the irradiant incident at the airport greatly strengthening my conviction that he would know what I should do.

"Baba Ram Dass, I really need some help and advice," I said. "I'm really worried about what's happening to me. I want to know if I'm going crazy. I'm having experiences in yoga class, like visions of the Himalayas, seeing lights, and auras and hearing divine sounds in my head. I'm walking around London with no weight in my body. It feels like only my boots are holding me to the ground!

"I keep going to yoga like it is an addiction. I have these experiences of rushing energy like orgasms in my body in class, and this beautiful music plays in my head day and night. And one time I saw this amazing thing - I saw my yoga teacher's aura! It was brilliant blue light around his head, and then superimposed on it were thousands of sparkling, shimmering golden streaks, I couldn't believe it, and it was so amazing it totally put me in shock, and bliss, and – I'm scared!"

Ram Dass (as he is now known) was just looking at me kindly and smiling encouragingly.

"When I am on location filming in gorgeous places in the Mediterranean all I want is to be alone to meditate and do yoga," I continued. "It's as if I am charmed, hypnotized, possessed. All I want to do is listen to this Kirtan, (sacred God- inspired music), this wonderful music playing in my head that my yoga teacher sings, it's there haunting me day and night. I don't want to see anyone or go out, no matter how interesting the sights or activities. I just want to stay in my hotel room listening to this heavenly music inside my head while everyone else goes out to dinner and discotheques. I know they think I'm crazy. Well, I agree, I think so too! And I wonder too because I usually love going dancing more than anything but now, you know, I don't even care what they think!"

His smiling eyes were radiant, full of light and sweetness, just looking and nodding understandingly, empathetically.

"Most of all I am really scared of my parents finding out. I really do care what they think. They would be so horrified. They would think he is so weird and they would be right, as he wears a turban and a long beard. They would worry I am getting brainwashed into a cult with a guru that just wants my money. I worry about that too, because we hear about it all the time, but I try to reassure myself because of the fact that he doesn't ask for a fee but teaches by donation."

Ram Dass was listening; appearing deeply focused, and then closed his eyes in meditation.

"My parents and everybody, I know they would think he's gone insane with a lifestyle of too much sex, drugs and rock 'n roll. Who would give up fame and fortune and touring the world, being a producer and arranger at Capitol Records in Hollywood, to then live like a penniless yogi like he seems to be doing? I mean, what a waste, you know?

"They really want me to be with decent respectable people and end up marrying a nice, rich, normal man and live at least a normal looking life. Of course, I understand and want to do the right thing by them, they are wonderful good parents and I love them very much and don't want to hurt them, but I worry, I know they will never understand.

"Also, the thing is, I have worked hard at my acting career, and it's on the verge of really taking off now. I don't want to give up my career, and I am afraid of what might happen if I keep spending time in the presence of people who are so, well, like my mother would say, "not normal!" Why I am so attracted to all this… what does it mean, and what should I do?"

Ram Dass sat in deep silence. I had never felt so listened to! It was an extraordinarily soul satisfying experience! Feeling myself embraced in such profound presence and peace, it was like he was listening to my very soul. No one had ever listened to my soul before. It was like being expanded into a vast space, and held in a field of delicious understanding and intimacy. The feeling was of a warmth and aliveness and "at oneness" in my body heart and soul, like, wow, what I had dreamt of and longed for all my life. Yes, this was a dream come true! It was soul connection, it was presence, the power of presence – wow, the unimaginable and indescribable was visiting me… ah, was this what I remembered at birth and was here to remember?

Finally he spoke, "Imagine if, for example, I were married to you…" At that, my heart leapt up! I'll never know how his sentence ended. My whole being was erupting in ecstasy inside, taking me over saying, "Yes! That's what I want! I want to be married to a holy man like you who is present like you and has the sun around his head!"

I was in shock at this unexpected experience. I had never thought of anything like this. Simultaneously I was thinking, why is marriage even mentioned, where did that come from? I have no interest in marriage, not to anybody or anything! I don't want marriage and children, I like my freedom. These are "burn-your-bra" Germaine Greer freedom times! I want to be a liberated, modern woman, not a bound-at-home-for-life housewife like my mother! Stop! Wait! No way am I giving up my life and career!

When I came back to earth and regained my senses and comprehension, I heard him saying, "Some of the highest beings I know are on the path of Kundalini Yoga, so why not you… leave behind the movie star and be a spiritual star. Go for it!"

I learned later that in India surrender to and merging with God is likened to marriage of the "soul-bride" to God the bridegroom and realized that Ram Dass was referring to the consciousness of commitment to surrendering up the ego-driven life for a spirit-driven life…as he had done.

After meeting Ram Dass and experiencing his incredible presence and his direction to "go for it" I was even more scared. But something big had happened to me, and how to "be here now" became the driving force of my life.

My interviews and pictures continued showing up in the papers, but there was a change. I spoke to the sometimes bemused journalists about yoga and service. The Western cultural paradigm of a human life focused on self and getting ahead materialistically, owning more, buying more and valuing self for how much, was, in my mind, now in question. One newspaper interview quoted me as saying, "I have lived such a selfish life…"

Instead of sexy outfits, tiny miniskirts, skin tight jumpsuits, 'hot pants', see-through crochet and diaphanous lace blouses, I was now photographed rather more covered up. My clothes were white with a little lace in the skirt and sleeves, my only concession to glamour. The fashionable heavy makeup and false eyelashes of the times were much less noticeable than previously.

Final photo shoot before leaving the entertainment world - 1972

One day I'm the only student to show up at yoga class. Vikram Singh asks me to massage his feet. I've learned that foot massage is part of Kundalini Yoga, but being nervous and shy, and afraid that I am not good enough at it, I feel scared he will discover I'm not a good student.

Worse yet, he might realize – I'm attracted to him!

"Go on!" he says now in his typical authoritative manner. I am very freaked out, but by now in the habit of obeying my teacher's instructions, my hand - all by itself - reaches out tentatively to make contact with his nearest foot....

Instantly like a lightning bolt of massive voltage an unknown energy shoots through my body, coursing through my whole being, shaking up my world, and - ending my life as I know it!

It sounds corny, I know. But it's happening, just like that! I don't know how, I know nothing! It's amazing, it's just happening; it's not me doing anything! It feels like all the forces of the universe are doing this, pushing us together! That's exactly how it is!

I'll never know how - there's no memory, it's just happening… now we are no longer sitting… We are somehow now standing. And close together. Neither of us moving of our own volition.

It's happening to us; we are doing nothing. And now we are even closer, all the forces of the universe are pushing us ever closer. Our arms reaching out, suddenly are finding each other… doing nothing, being done to, our lips are meeting...

7

Falling In Love

*All the Forces of Heaven and Earth
*Agonizing Inner Conflicts *Vikram Singh's
Decision *"I'll be Right Back!" *Leaving for
Los Angeles*

And so began our strange and harrowing courtship dance. Although our desire to be together was almost unbearable our worlds were very different. Vikram Singh knew the world of entertainment very well and knew how addictive it was, almost impossible to extract oneself from. For my part, even though I was so disturbed about many things in my world, I was experiencing an intoxicating success and felt there was plenty more to come.

It was not until many years later that Vikram – by this time, Antion – was able to express to me how agonizing it had been for him. In his world, marriage was a duty, to be decided and even arranged by his teacher. Falling in love was frowned upon and the idea of falling for a flighty, flirtatious sex-symbol was totally beyond the pale. Thus he felt that – by feeling so strongly attracted to me – that he was betraying his principles and his commitment to his teacher. He could not see how it would be possible for me to walk away from such a promising career to face a future with him that was at best uncertain.

I also never realized how hard it was for him just being in the UK. Although he was born and brought up not too far from London, his few brief years in California had brought out his American blood and he had literally become a Californian. It was a real life manifestation of the Eagles' song, *Hotel California*, even though it had not yet been written: "You can check out any time you like, but you can never leave".

His body had moved from Los Angeles to London but his spirit remained in Southern California. To him, London felt like an alien world with its cynical conservative attitudes and – above all – its miserable weather.

To add to all this uncertainty, Vikram received a letter from the Yogi telling him that he was to be engaged to a woman in Los Angeles. I was surprised when I heard about this. My world was changing, what was going on? I didn't know what to make of it, which made me feel strange, vulnerable and insecure.

I didn't know it but the stress of our unfulfilled relationship, the frustration of being somewhere where he felt totally out of place and now being told he was "engaged" to someone towards whom he had no desire or interest was becoming too much for him. He wrote to the Yogi to ask if he could return to Los Angeles. "Come home" was the simple reply.

One day after class one of my yoga classmates drew me aside and asked me if he could meet with me, and we agreed to go to my favorite place in Hyde Park close to my home. I loved nature, the trees, and the lake, and welcomed every excuse to go there.

Yoga friends - Graham is second from right

Graham was my favorite yoga friend, I had come to like this earnest Englishman, and to trust him. So now why was he staring at me in this disconcertingly serious manner? "You know our teacher Vikram Singh is leaving for California in a few weeks".

My world was spinning. He knew…he was still staring into my eyes. He had to deliver his message. "I think you should go to Los Angeles with him".

Trying to act nonchalant I opened my mouth, but nothing came out. "I'll tell him you want to go. Would you like me to help arrange it?"

"No, no!" Finding my voice, "No way. I can't imagine getting ready in that short time. I have important things to do, an audition for a new role, plus a confirmed role, my best yet. I can't just up and leave. No way. And what about my house, I can't just leave that either. No, it's just impossible."

It was nothing but a mere suggestion, so why did it hit me like a bombshell? I staggered home practically trembling with a wild mixture of fear, anxiety, conflict and excitement. I tried but couldn't stop the feelings; my mind was reeling, going wild.

Then from nowhere a thought slipped into my awareness. "But, wait… could I? Might it be possible? What if I made a very quick trip…surely it wouldn't do any harm. I could tell my agents (I had one for modeling as well as for acting) that I'll be right back…"

I was terrified of these dangerous thoughts and tried to block them out. It felt like I was standing on one of these petrifying now-or-never brinks. I was feeling that familiar adventurous pull to jump into the unknown. Could I do it? At the same time I was truly scared… what might happen to me? I didn't dare think about it, I tried to dismiss the questions.

The flight he was booked on was April 22, in two weeks. Days passed in total inner turmoil…until, well, one day I found myself packing a suitcase.

Thus somehow, I don't know how, the decision was made; the flight booked. And then an interesting thing happened. I watched myself doing this even as I wondered why. After all, I had no intention of doing anything after this trip but getting back to London, back to my career as fast as possible. After all, I just wanted to go to Los Angeles to meet my teacher's teacher. That was it.

But secretly, at the back of my mind, I was playing with the desire to take a yoga teacher training. I had found a talent for yoga; after the initial stiffness of those first weeks it felt natural and easy and I was really good at it, very attracted and yearning to learn more. In those days as far as the camera and modeling and movies was concerned, you were considered old at age 22! Secretly I wanted a career that would ensure a more lasting future, one that had nothing to do with my looks.

So why did I pack my portfolio of photos, hiding them at the bottom of my suitcase? I didn't want to think it - or anything - through…But… I had to wonder, why did I do that? Did some part of me think I might not get back to London … or was it thinking I was actually going to California to further my career there? Or was it insurance in case I needed it, in case something went wrong, and I would be alone there needing to make a living as an actress/model/movie star? Or was this just in case someone would 'discover' me there, as had happened in London?

I wondered about the contradictory parts of me wanting different things. I wasn't in control, and didn't even know who I was. Yet somehow it didn't matter, my life was unfolding beyond my control. I had always felt that yes, the world was at my feet; I could do and have whatever I wanted, and what I wanted and had to have was something, I didn't know what, but it was big, really big. I had read "Think and Grow Rich" when I was 15, about how if you put your mind to it you could manifest anything.

And now there was this part of me that wanted the approval of my yoga teacher. I was letting his teachings have influence over me. If he said to wear white clothes then that is what I wanted to do. Knowing what the ideal was - hair up in a topknot, white not tight but rather shapeless clothes designed to take consciousness up and away from the lower chakras. Using only natural fibers, not synthetic, were part of the lifestyle teachings; wear cotton, wool, silk or rayon, not toxic chemicals that affected your skin and magnetic field.

One day I decided to try it, and so showed up at yoga class dressed in similar fashion to the American yogis, hair up in a knot, feeling really weird, strange and shocked at myself...but proud too...and in suspense longing for his approval...the almost imperceptible but faintly approving glance and nod from him was just enough to put me into an ecstasy! How ridiculous...

Yes, but still, my inner rebel didn't want to do what others prescribed. This part wanted to hold out and not be a follower. It decided I just had to retain some individuality. So what to wear for the trip was a dualistic dilemma.

I had this brilliantly colored canary yellow zipped up long fur fluffy jacket, and wanted to wear it purely because it was so outrageous. I rationalized that yellow was close to white in color. In spite of being a very shy child and teenager, maybe because of it, I loved inadvertently (I was such a goody-goody so would never do it deliberately!) scandalizing and shocking conservative people, and so decided this is what I had to wear for the trip.

But what else to wear with it? I was used to shopping in trendy King's Road and Carnaby Street; I loved the wildly creative stuff. I actually had clothes, pants, tailored at a men's store in Carnaby Street where the best most innovative tailors competed to create the latest wildest fashions. In those days you had to be in fashion at the threat of being shamed, you just had to! I loved the famous designer Ossie Clark's transparent blouses and had one with this crazy dinosaur frill up the arms.

Conveniently the Indian-look with cotton gauze was high fashion, so I found this dress of strong bright canary yellow gauze. As if that weren't enough, it was tiered with layers of audacious very bright red and purple frills.

So there I was, dressed for this trip in a way designed to shock and declare my independence - at least to try to retain some semblance of independence - while simultaneously looking as if I were obediently catering to the Indian look. In retrospect my choice of exactly these colors was an instinctive attempt to power up my energy field and chakras for the challenges ahead!

We left London from Luton airport at midnight on a Boeing 707. Although the plane was full we had three seats between the two of us, unusual on that type of flight. It seemed as if the Universe was supporting our togetherness. Even though we were trying to not touch each other, and to hide our mutual attraction, we fell asleep leaning on each other in a very intimate fashion. When I awoke, we had crossed the Atlantic and were flying over the vast North American Continent in the warm light of early morning.

Hour after hour my face remained glued to the window, in wonder, absolutely entranced by the brilliant ever blue skies we flew through, looking down over endless vast stretches of land and mountains and rivers. My soul was deeply touched, never having even imagined anything like this display of magnificent nature. Mountains, fields, gorges, winding rivers and roads, all were creating an incomparable tapestry of breathtaking beauty of God's creation.

I was thrilled by my first sight of California and then Los Angeles. Like some space ship the huge airport and dome radiated whiteness in the shining bright Californian sun and brilliant sky. The scene was unforgettable, setting the tone for what was to come.

8

Los Angeles – Meeting the Yogi

*Culture shock! *Fear of Commitment *The World at Their Feet They Kicked It Away! *Getting Married *Speak with One Voice*

Exiting Customs and Immigration, we beheld a wondrous scene: at the foot of the stairs was a great sea of whiteness; an enormous crowd of chanting faces, all there to meet my celebrated yoga teacher.

In spite of my outfit of bold colors with lipstick and shoes to match, my self-confidence began to wane in the face of this enthusiastic greeting, as mellifluous singing wafted up to greet and surround us. I was disconcerted to find myself separated from Vikram. One of the white dressed women beckoned me to follow her to her car, where she motioned for me to get in, never pausing in the stream of chant issuing from her mouth. She never asked me my name, never talked to me, simply chanted the whole time we were driving. I was astonished, in shock. When we reached our destination I was greeted at the door by more smiling, chanting women who had food ready for us. While it was being laid out one sweet-faced, kind devotee massaged my feet in an expert and thorough way.

We were invited to seat ourselves on cushions around a long low table offering an all-vegetarian feast delightful to all eyes and senses: baked casseroles, stuffed potatoes, vegetables and yams, steamed broccoli, lentil loaf, varieties of tofu dishes, fresh colorful salads with rich dressings, a choice of numerous grains and selection of sauces, fresh baked breads and muffins, and everything bountifully served up on enormous plates.

It was my first introduction to the typically wholesome, all organic and delectable food made by these health and food loving chanting devotees - and it was impressive! For me this was food culture shock! It was so different from the way people ate in Britain. I had been raised on superb Danish food grown in clean, green New Zealand and considered my mother one of the best cooks in the world. So what was it about this food that was so way over the top special and delicious?

It must have been the sheer energy in the food. It was so alive! Maybe the explosion of consciousness within the flower-power hippie movement had engendered a revolution in food.

And it was more than that! I figured out that above all the secret must be in how the food was prepared. It must be all of that plus the inspired chanting with what they were calling "group consciousness" focus.

Then came desserts, oh my! again selections of fruit pies and ice creams like I had never tasted, and this was a first, my first taste of a health food meal in itself, a smoothie, a healthy creatively blended selection of fresh fruits and various super-foods, protein powders and supplements such as spirulina, bee pollen lecithin etc. I knew there was nothing like this in the whole world. And there still isn't, even though the rest of the world is trying to catch up.

Afterwards we were brought to another house by more chanting, white-clad people, and each given a room. It was a very white ashram set in what I found out (much) later was West Hollywood, one of the trendiest neighborhoods in LA. It was newly painted, very simple and very clean. My room had a mattress on the wood floor, the bed made up. There were no carpets, few curtains, very simple.

Still no one had spoken to me in a personal way. They just chanted. I was struck with the incongruity of all this. My movie star persona and every other persona I had come to identify with – the academic genius, the scholar researcher, the top ballroom dancer, the top model, the actress, the nature-lover survivalist - were all being totally ignored.

There was just me, me very alone in this almost empty very white room, this all white chanting environment. Me in my yellow outfit. The bright yellow stood out as never before, as did the red and purple layers of my tiered frilly dress, the whiteness of my surrounding walls reflecting the contrasting brightness. Just me alone with my suitcase. The contents reflecting my split consciousness, the duality and polarity. On the top were the very conservative white Indian yogi type clothes representing virginal modesty and purity, and beneath, hidden at the bottom, my secret life. My portfolio of glamorous and sexy pictures. My very expensive, sexy, handmade, see-through crocheted silver chain blouse from Paris, worn open at the front to reveal semi-naked breasts. What was I thinking? Was this me? Were there perhaps two me's?

Nobody asked me, nobody cared. All this was mind-boggling, almost like landing on another planet.

When I had first arrived in England the English accent was such I could not understand what people were saying, nor could I distinguish individual voices one from another. Here again the voices around me sounded all the same, whether chanting or speaking, all with American accents I could not understand. I noticed that most speech - that was not chanted - was prefaced with the words, "The Yogi says"… to do this or that etc. The yogic teaching was to live in a meditative consciousness which meant talk less, - keep talking to a minimum, - to develop group consciousness, in order to break the identification with your past, with your belief systems.

I found out that it was considered a great privilege to get to see "The Yogi" privately. I immediately made an appointment to see him as soon as possible. The great day came; I was excited I would be meeting someone very extraordinary like I had read about in Yogananda's book, a spiritual master, a guru, a yogi, a saint.

I had read about Yogananda finding his teacher, and my longings were stirred for a great teacher who would recognize and value me, my spirit and my good qualities. He would guide me to my greater spirituality, to find and live what my path was in this world. Like the honorable and noble Sri Yukteswar had guided and taught Yogananda on the spiritual path. At last I was to meet my ultimate teacher, the one I had secretly sought since discovering Yogananda's book as a teenager.

I wanted to trust, I wanted something true and powerful and real to believe in, and I yearned to throw myself into whatever might bring me to fulfillment of this mysterious longing inside me. I wanted someone to know about me, my life and what was best for me - because I didn't. The only thing I had figured out about life was that the purpose of mine was to chalk up experiences, I didn't know for what, but hoped it would one day all fall into place. I hoped that life would acquire personal meaning - not my parents' version - worthy though that might be – but my own.

I thought about my life, reflecting on what the Yogi would see, remembering that from the time of my birth I had eagerly sought the meaning of life. I hungered for learning, felt like everything presented to me I already knew. I gulped down the contents of every single book that came my way: books were my best friends; they went with me at all times. From birth in Denmark to becoming top of the class in a new language in my first year at school in New Zealand and remaining there throughout my school years, I excelled in languages, sports and dancing. After five years at university I had the world at my feet as they say, but didn't know where they were leading me. Academia and intellectuality no longer excited me, disillusionment prevailed, but still I was full of idealistic dreams and longings. What did it all mean?

I imagined the Yogi would be sitting on the floor, - well, not exactly on a bed of nails! - But at least in simple surroundings, on a wooden floor, simple and sacred, with his eyes rolled up in deep meditation, like the saints and sages Yogananda described. I was already envisioning what I wanted and expected of a holy man guru. He would listen to me as Ram Dass had done. He would direct my longings for the spiritual path with the hallmarks of truth: integrity, authenticity, and trustworthiness.

I was in for a shock. This was a worldly scene, the room luxuriously appointed, not at all the austere and simple place I was expecting and envisioning. His energy and appearance was like nothing I had ever seen, a huge man with piercing dark eyes lounging in a robe in a great armchair with an air like he owned the world, you, me and everything else.

He didn't greet me, shake hands, ask how I was; he just stared for a moment then made utterance with: "Premka is beautiful too, you know" referring to his chief secretary. What? I was shocked that these were his very first words, words referring to feminine attractiveness. How could this be, just like any other man! That was not what I was there for. And why compare me to somebody else?

"Why do you cut your hair?" came next, which made no sense to me either. In shock I thought, "What? What on earth could be the matter with my hair?" Then, "How many men have you slept with?"

I had never been spoken to like that before. Why this imperious questioning and implied disapproval of my appearance and private life? Why would he bring up men and sex? I remembered as a young girl in NZ instinctively valuing virginity and being determined to stay a virgin until I was married. Even back then that idea was ridiculous to most women, so it was a lonely and secret stance. I valued and guarded my innocence, and it had nothing to do with religion as I didn't have any. As for sex, what I had experienced so far was disillusionment.

I sat, numb, dumb, shocked and paralyzed. It was the very opposite of the way Ram Dass had treated me. Here there was no listening, no interest in who I was, what I might have to say. I felt horribly unnerved, like I was being stripped bare. I thought my longings would be acknowledged and honored, but instead – this was a whole new experience and I didn't like it, and didn't know what to make of it.

Then suddenly, fiercely, he said, "I want your head!"

"What"?!! Desperate thoughts surged racing through my mind, "Oh my God, I've made a terrible mistake! I've got to get out of here, thank God I know those Sufis and that film director, I can run to them, and they'll help me to the airport. This is a total phony, a fake, just out for control, money and power, just like my parents and people have warned me, and I know it now. What a mistake to come here!" Thousands of such frantic thoughts of speedy escape continued racing through my mind. You know how we hear of people in crisis under threat or accident believing their end has come, how their whole life runs before their eyes like a movie, that's how it was!

But then a strange thing happened. I started remembering stories in mythology of ancient times where the hero has to overcome great odds, challenges, obstacles, great monsters and darkness and evil that is opposing him, while simultaneously conquering inner fears, weaknesses, self-importance and pride. Only then would the reward be forthcoming, the prince or princess's eternal love, the Holy Grail, freedom, enlightenment.

Could this be a test, the "hero's test"? After all, both Ram Dass and Vikram Singh had led me here, and I trusted them. So... So it must be all right? I rationalized wildly that if my yoga teacher (whom I did trust) and all these other people thought this man was in integrity, he must be. Ram Dass had sent me in this direction. And he knew what was good for me, because he was a renowned author, supposedly a holy man, and many people thought so, and he was famous, and most of all, I myself had seen his brilliant aura with my own eyes, and so it must be true... my desperate reasoning went on.

I had recently been reading a book about enlightenment written by a woman saint. Suddenly I was remembering her words, something like this, "The key to liberation from ego is to find a hook - it doesn't really matter what it is - on which to hang up your ego".

From some faraway place I heard a voice, my voice? This voice said, "Okay".

"Dress like my secretary and walk with Vikram Singh to the ashram every morning for sadhana".

Horrors, it was my voice. How could it say okay like that? I was done for. I would have to accept it, take it as such; this must be "the hook" on which to "hang my ego". Yes, I was being challenged and so my confused and benumbed instinctive response was to step up to the challenge. This must be what I wanted in some part of me. Moreover, the Yogi acted like he knew all about me, my soul, my destiny, and I wanted someone to do that, and I really wanted to replace my inner uncertainty and confusion with - if not my own then somebody's! - conviction. I wanted from somewhere a non-negotiable absolute authority.

The outfit I was ordered to dress in was a white long loose cotton top called a kurta with big baggy loose pants called churidars. So I acquired this strange dress, a bit like a uniform. Because I had only the one outfit, and I wore it all the time, I had to wash it every night before I went to bed, which was at about 10pm. Then I had to wait 45 minutes for it to wash, so as to get it into the dryer, so that it would be ready to take out and iron when I got up a few hours later at 2.30am in the morning. I had to be on time to fulfill my assignment to walk for an hour and arrive at the main ashram for Sadhana at 4am.

One night I had another mind-blowing experience. As usual I was dealing with the washing and drying of my clothes, this time at midnight, when I noticed a man named Baba Singh working, sanding down one of the doors in the ashram. I wondered why he would work during the day, come home and work some more in the middle of the night doing something nobody would even notice and appreciate, he wasn't being paid to do, and which would not benefit him personally in any way since he didn't even own the house.

Something unexpected happened in my heart. It was an experience: that self I had spent years building up and identifying with was suddenly losing its self-important significance in the face of this unexpected glimpse of devotion and selflessness.

Every morning at 3:30 am, without speaking, Vikram Singh and I headed out the door together as ordered, and embarked on another day of uncertainty, striding along in this uneasy silence not knowing what would become of our strange relationship. In spite of this situation, there was an excitement and magic for me in being here in Los Angeles in California in the great USA. It was similar to what I had felt when I first landed in

London. Coming from the British winter, the warmth, atmosphere and vibration of springtime LA was thrilling.

On one of these mornings we were stopped by the police. "What are you doing out at this ungodly hour?" It was laughable, so completely ironic. There we were on a pilgrimage to enlightenment in the streets of LA in the early morning darkness, obeying the teacher's commands. Walking in our white-garbed discipline, striding towards the dawn, we were looking for God, while they, the police, were looking for criminals.

I knew whatever we said would sound ridiculous, as we already looked highly unusual. So I held back my impulse to say, "Well, I don't really know why I am here walking along Melrose Avenue at 3.30 in the morning together with a man who was my yoga teacher in London. I seem to be undergoing a test from a spiritual teacher. He ordered me to walk three miles at this hour of morning dressed like this, he really is testing me, but he teaches that this is not an ungodly hour but in fact a very godly hour indeed to meditate and do yoga, and so I am on my way to do that, and am trying to feel it as well because I want to believe him because I am lost and want to believe in something in this weird world."

I thought of my dawn sojourn to the ashram in London, for me the spirit was similar, this was my next step on the spiritual path. And that was why I was here, here where we could as a group movement in group consciousness move mountains to change the world. I felt in the early morning air the smells of vegetation and flowers opening, the thrill of being in the forefront as pioneers of consciousness creating a whole new world. That world would be one where truth, love, security, kindness, sweetness and goodness reigned supreme and sacred.

We would arrive at the ashram and start with some yoga, then a do a few hours of meditating followed by singing. This was a sacred time, the ambrosial hour. I felt within me and in the atmosphere of discipline that anything was possible by the power of meditation.

At 6.30 am the private door to the Yogi's quarters would open up and he would join us from his inner rooms, taking charge, directing the music and drumming. I loved the spirited high energy singing, chanting and drumming and often afterwards a secretary delivered a personal message for us. He wanted to see us in his back rooms. He would regale us with his will, talking about how we should get married. His secretaries and grown children might also be present, I would protest, and they would laugh.

I would repeat, "I have to get back to my life in London, my agents are waiting for me and I am just visiting here, and expecting to go to take teachers training in Phoenix. Yes, I do feel I love him; I will always carry a picture of this man, for the rest of my life and travels,   plus listen to his Kirtan. To me he is a great inspiration; to me he is the great, holy Vikram Singh. But marriage to him seems impossible, unthinkable. I also have promised to visit my parents in NZ. They have been waiting for me far too long already."

I was obligated. I owed it to them to go back, for their sake. And if I was going to think of marriage, I owed it to them   to marry someone they would consider worth marrying, that is someone propertied with assets and connections.

"And another thing is", I said, "I am afraid of his devotion. I am afraid of marrying a religious fanatic. I love his music, but he has these symbols of commitment with him all the time, - this sword and special underwear - and will probably never even take them off to sleep."

 This went on for a few weeks or so, while I am continuing to think, "No, not for me the limitations of marriage, after all I am an up and coming actress, a woman's liberationist, a philosopher, a learned connoisseur of literature, art and architecture, giving interviews, having significant things to say, a survivalist of determination who successfully breezed across icy faces of cliffs with sheer drops to chasms miles below, when others slipped and died...."

At one point he said, "I want you to come to me for private lessons." He was flattering me, catering to my longing to be special, courting me. I liked the attention. I kept repeating how I needed to return soon to London, while they all laughed. It was a game that was fast drawing to an end.

I admired and respected Vikram Singh for his devotion and commitment to his own teacher. At these times he seemed withdrawn, unlike himself, but then I barely knew him except as a yoga teacher telling me what it do in class. I had no recognizable, real relationship with him. I had no inkling of what he was going through, that he was trying to hold back and was filled with guilt to be in love with someone without prior permission and approval from his teacher. But I felt his great unease and misery at the situation. Something had to give.

One day, in dark tones, Vikram announced that he wanted to speak to me.

"The Yogi told me to forget all about you."

I knew right way he had made up his mind to do so. The game was up. I knew who came first in his life. And it wasn't me. A contrast indeed from all those men who were always falling all over themselves for me. I knew he loved me and wanted me. But still he was giving me up. He would sacrifice this love for obedience to one he respected more than me, more than himself; the one he loved more than me.

I felt his uncompromising withdrawal like an icy, solid wall dropping between us. Shaking inside, in shock, my world was collapsing. This was my yoga teacher who represented a lifestyle of devotion to a non-materialistic life, whose ashram was open to all who would come for food, help, advice, whose music resonated in my soul day and night, in whose classes I had ecstatic visions of Guru Nanak raining gold on me, classes which had put me in such bliss I could no longer enjoy even my exotic life of glamour and material glory. He whose values had ensnared me with the joy of truth, so that I would rush home from every movie or modeling assignment just to be able to go and chant again in that simple, orange carpeted room in Notting Hill.

This was my yoga teacher who all the forces of the universe had brought me closer to, who had asked the universe for a "good woman", and most of all, with whom I had fallen in love. My independent stand and stance of "I don't need anyone", was being challenged, all my fences around my idealistic soul which had dreamed from the time of birth for a knight-in-shining amour, trembled in shock. I know he loves me and wants me! A terrible confusion came over me as I felt my mind clouding over.

Then something surprising happened, another thought and energy put in an appearance. From some unknown place, it was as if a part of me opened up a long slumbering eye, with the question, is it possible oh world, that there is space for me here, to live, after all?

Could I show myself, awaken from my long dead sleep in this world? Is there hope after all? Like the story I had heard of – in the time of Socrates

– thousands of years before of one who had wandered around with a lamp lit in the middle of the day. When people asked, "What are you doing?" he answered, "Looking for an honest man!" I had looked a long time, could this be a true man, an honest man? Could such a one be found?

And from another place in me, instant rebuttal, no, no. it is impossible to allow the dream to awaken. Absolutely not. There is no such man, and not for me. And if I believed, it would cost me. Too much.

This was the end. I would simply depart for the teacher training in Phoenix and return to England after that. Decision made, I was calm, mind made up.

After sadhana the Yogi was there. So I thought I should let him know I was going.

"I have arranged a ride with friends to Phoenix, I am leaving this morning". He said "I love you. Write to me every day". He fixed me with an inscrutable expression, staring into my eyes. My legs tried to stand up to leave, but did not succeed. They were not raising me up; they did not obey my intention to get up and walk out. My gut was a hollow vacuum. I stared back at him.

Quite casually he looked away. I was still trying to get up; my continuing and only intention was to stand up from my sitting position on the floor and leave. But for once in my life I was not in control. My legs were simply not moving. I never knew what happened and to this day I don't know. All I know is that I found myself speaking, well, at least words were issuing from my mouth, only they were not words that came from my own volition… I think these words were, "I would like to do what you think would be best".

Like a volcano the whole world was erupting and exploding! And I was falling, falling, like off a terrifying precipice that was collapsing down, down, spinning, spinning, falling down. A gigantic roar was filling the room, "Veeeeekraaaaaaaaam!!!

Vikram had already left. He was outside, sitting on the curb, lacing up his boots. For him the painful drama was over. He had just taken his first obedient, relief-filled step out of my life. Hearing his teacher's shouted command he took off his boots again and reappeared in the room.

I was in shock. "Oh no, God no, I'm done for, what a frightful mistake, I've got to reverse this, I must escape this consequence of my words, heeeaalp!"

Still in a roaring voice, "You want to marry this woman?" The whole room held its breath - dramatic silence. Forty people were watching this spectacle in fascinated stillness.

This man had already suffered a lot of confusion guilt and pain over me, and wanted no more, and now he was being put on the spot big time. Pinned down, paralyzed, this was massive public humiliation. Whatever the outcome, either way it would be life-changing.

Humiliation beyond belief. And what if he said yes? And what if he said no? The universe stood still. Suspended over a chasm, a void, all eternity. Long, infinitely long, bated-breath quiet. Finally, the word, "Yes."

I was absolutely freaked at this turn of events. Suddenly I was being committed under orders to marriage! To a spiritual fanatic who had made it very clear through his conscious choices that I was only 4th down the line in his allegiance, loyalty and affections. First came God, then Guru, then Teacher, then, finally...me.

I sat horrified, desperately wanting to run away. I wanted to protest, explain, yell, wail, "Wait, wait, there's been a mistake! This can't be happening, no, no, I didn't mean it! It's not what I want, no, no, no, help, this is all too fast!"

This was not the way I had dreamed of my ultimate union with my knight-in-shining-amour, my soul mate that would one day appear! I thought we were supposed to meet in a field of waving golden grasses and we would fall into each other's arms in instant recognition and communicate in ancient tongues of intimacy having known each other forever...in total agreement telepathically, and adore each other above all, and eat ice cream to our heart's content for the rest of our days.

I had good reason to be truly terrified. This would not be marriage to a man. This would be marriage to commitment. To duty. To obedience. To sacrifice. To strictness. To inflexibility. To honor. To missionary zeal. To a chanting religious fanatic. And most likely personal misery for the sake of service to a cause, a cause always and ever more important than me as a person. I was down the line in importance, only 4th in line.

It wasn't for nothing that my teachers called me "self- effacing" on my report cards, now I was proving it, this was crazy! This was self-sacrifice, and even beyond, self-annihilation! I must be crazy!

"Get the papers and blood test. You'll be married here by me next Monday after sadhana." The room broke into a huge roar of approval. Everyone cheered! I found myself staggering out of there in a benumbed state of shock being mobbed by all these over-excited people.

Here we were, one second we were each going our own ways, the next we were bound together as a 'we' in an arranged marriage, which obviously we could never have come to ourselves, not in a million years no!

In that moment of finding myself on the pavement outside the ashram standing stunned in total disbelief, trying to grok that I was now 'we', that somehow 'I' had become 'we', we didn't know how to relate to anything, or what to do next. We stood side by side helplessly in a state of shock while everybody showered us with happy congratulations.

Worlds turned and rolled over; I was spinning through the universe. But here in this body, even while feeling appalled and beside myself with apprehension, yet another feeling was taking over. How could this be? Somehow in spite of the inner turmoil, something unusual was happening, somewhere inside me oddly like a settling... oh my, even a relief! I became aware that that horrible hollow vacuum of emptiness in my gut was gone. It was being replaced with something, something that felt like a fullness, almost like a sense of inevitability...maybe destiny coming to right fulfillment. It felt a bit like...what it might feel like to find some long lost something you were looking for...oh, yes, maybe even like a shipwrecked sailor on the point of death sighting land!

In spite of that strange sense of (temporary) peace, the ensuing week was a wild roller coaster of fear and turmoil, and getting cold feet and trying to back out. I thought about running away, but to do what and go where? I fantasized about disappearing to look for the movie director or those Sufis I had heard about.

And still I wanted to go to Phoenix for teacher training, catch a ride with the guys who were preparing to leave. I found myself organizing it, deciding I just had to go with them. And I would just tell him, he who was my newly committed—under-pressure fiancé, I would just inform him, "Look, I just have to go; you know that's why I came to LA!"

All hell broke loose; he lost his temper, he blew up, he went nuts! And in the public courtyard of the ashram where we were staying, right there in the open, in public and all, there we were shamefully engaging in a great yelling match. In the end, he grabbed me in a head lock, and pressing my arm up behind my back shrieked loudly, "Will you marry me or not?"

Forced to double up, with the pain increasing, knees buckling, "You bastard! Let me go!" I screamed at the top of my lungs.

"Shaddap! Will you marry me or not?"

Knees almost on the ground, dressed in my white ego-erasing-spiritual-uniform, with no further down to go, what could I do? I had to say it. I shrieked, "Yes, "Yes". And he let me go and helped me to my feet.

I realized I had actually never said 'yes' until then. And the Yogi had not asked me the question. He assumed that my surrender to his will for me meant my assent to marriage...or whatever! So this was my marriage proposal and this was my response, yelling from my knees on the ground in pain!

Oh, but I still couldn't let it go, my desire to go to teacher training. I just had to go; I was determined to get to Phoenix. Now he was at his wits end. So he put in a desperate call to the Yogi to tell him I was trying to run away, what should he do? Remarkably, the Yogi promptly returned the call, demanded to speak to me, got me on the phone, and laughed and laughed in my ear. I was so astonished that somehow the wind was taken out of my sails, until it all seemed quite funny even to me. It was arranged that I would go later to the teacher training course in Phoenix.

Later that day Vikram proposed to me in a more formal and romantic fashion. This time I was not on my knees being coerced, maybe he was on his knees this time? And so I freely said yes, although still not without deep trepidation.

The day of my marriage dawned, 11th May 1972. I was up getting ready long before the dawn. It felt so inevitable but still scary. All thoughts of my future just erased. All thoughts of my past, gone. I belonged only to this moment. These white dressed women whom I had never really spoken with and so I did not even know took charge. They dressed me in a sari. They brought roses from somewhere and crowned my head with them. Someone even produced a garter belt (blue to satisfy the tradition of "something borrowed something blue"). I pulled this thing over my foot and up my thigh laughing at the incongruity, why this tradition, and what did it mean to me? Especially given everything else about this marriage that was already so incomprehensible and out of my hands.

And yet most strangely of all, it somehow still felt more right than my first carefully planned and orchestrated traditional church wedding. (Oops, I wouldn't want to hurt my parents, they might read this, even though they're both deceased!).

The ceremony had begun and was part way through when the Yogi suddenly said, "Stop!" We froze. The audience froze; it had inhaled with a huge cosmic gasp and was holding its breath. The Yogi was highly intimidating at any time, so this was downright scary.

"Right now we're stopping everything. There's something you must do. We will not proceed any further with this marriage until you do it."

"Speak with one voice."

The Yogi was rarely quiet, so it was utterly disquieting to experience this sudden charged and expectant silence. His eyes closed, he just waited as if prepared to do so forever. As it became obvious nothing further was going to happen until – what? We didn't know! We were stuck, on the spot.

You know, it's a horrible feeling to feel something is expected of you, but you don't know what… So we had to come up with something, and it had to be the right answer, the answer he was looking for and waiting for. Lengthening silence, embarrassment and anxiety growing. How do I get around this, how survive this challenge? What to say?

Staring desperately, helplessly across at Vikram who looked equally flabbergasted, a thousand thoughts of doubt flooding my mind, oh God, does this mean I am making a big mistake? What do you mean, how do you "speak with one voice?" What does that mean? Why was the Yogi saying this? Did it mean we were supposed to merge somehow? He was always talking about a couple being "one soul in two bodies". How do you do that, what does that look like, especially right now right here in public in front of everybody? Do you have to think the same thing at the same time and then say it? And oh my God, what if I don't get it right? How horrible and embarrassing and shameful to be shown up as unable to have the intellect or guts to rise to the occasion...

I sat paralyzed. In the spotlight, only this was a spotlight more intimidating and challenging than any I had ever experiences as an actress on stage or screen. Then Vikram Singh came to the rescue, came up with something we could speak together, he whispered it to me, something like 'yes we agree', so we pronounced it together to the audible relief - and growing hilarity of the audience, - and the ceremony continued to its conclusion.

Outside the Ashram, after the wedding - May 11th 1972, Los Angeles

Someone took group pictures of us afterwards, out in the street in front of the ashram. We look totally exhausted in those pictures, no sleep for days, bags under eyes, but interestingly (as pictures show so much), these pictures do carry a kind of beautiful innocent touching self-sacrificing air...of a sweet idealistic group of people giving up their personal lives in order to pursue and believe in something bigger than themselves, something they are convinced can change the world for the better.

When one of the pictures showed up recently on Facebook we were astonished it was receiving so many approving and delighted 'likes' and comments, even from people we had never even heard of. Maybe it struck a chord of nostalgia in some, of more innocent times...

Afterwards we left for a trip to the desert for our honeymoon, which was a good thing and a good start given that 17 years would pass before we again would take a vacation. I found a phone booth and called my parents in New Zealand. "Hi, Mum and Dad. I got married. He has a long beard and a turban - and a house". I knew mum would hate the first two items, but the house part at least she could accept. In her eyes a man with a house was very different from a man with no house.

I loved my parents and was greatly attached to my mother, along with her suffering at being separated from her large loving family in Denmark; I felt responsible and like her, deeply sentimental over the family we had left behind in Denmark. She didn't talk about it but I think she longed for them all her life. And so having left her and NZ I felt duty bound to return to NZ for similar reasons.

She was totally self-sacrificing and devoted to her family. It was not a conscious decision but I had long ago determined to be as unlike her as possible. Probably because I was like her, having plenty of fear and shyness. But I needed and wanted to be different. I wanted my own life and if ever I had children I would want to support them to have their own life. I could not pretend my life would never be about a comfortable life; at all costs I had to pursue what was in my heart and soul.

I knew my parents would be shocked, what an about-face from my life in London! I reflected on my mother's attachment to me. The fact that she was a superb housekeeper, seamstress and cook made no difference. I wanted something different out of life. She was unread, left school at age 14 to go to work, and so was insecure about herself; in her whole life she had only one job outside the home, so she lacked confidence in the world, and felt inadequate speaking her second language English. She sewed her own clothes and ours, always looked beautiful, had enormous strength and courage and was much loved by her family, and greatly admired by the community of Danes. For her there was no such thing as rest. She was a highly virtuous housewife, incredibly hardworking, and received little or no help with the housework from her three children and husband. She loved me, her life was about her children, and her own personal needs came last.

So much so that I actually thought she would accept all my changes. Little did I know I would never be back to New Zealand to live in her lifetime, and that my mother would never be able to accept my spiritual life and my turbaned bearded husband. At the time I simply expected my parents to do so. It never occurred to me that with this marriage she would lose her 'only daughter' yet again, and in an even more profound way.

We returned from our Palm Springs honeymoon with no idea of what to do next, where to go, how to live, what to do. We stayed at the same Ashram, only there was no room, and so we made our home on a foam pad on the floor of a big filthy dirty cobweb- covered garage with oil and muck on the floor, crammed with tools and gardening stuff and junk in every square foot, and hanging everywhere. In spite of that after one night I found myself saying to my new husband, "Funny thing, I thought this was a dirty old garage, but now it feels like a palace to me".

It didn't occur to me to question this drastic downsizing from a life of palatial international jet setting through exotic plush hotels and being in demand making hundreds or thousands of dollars per hour to a life with no house or furniture or savings or job or place to live or future. A simple silver band was my wedding ring created on the spot by a jewelry maker living in the Tucson desert for $7.

Rags to riches, riches to rags, what did it matter? Buddha had left his worldly life to find enlightenment. It all made sense from some part of my inner being. I was coming from the perspective that my soul was guiding this show and so it had to be this way.

I felt that we as a human race were on the verge of a great shift in consciousness; this was an inner conviction that guided my life. It meant a lot to me and if it meant sacrifices then so be it. This involved putting something bigger than me in the driver's seat. This was how it looked for now, and I had to do it. And that involved having to be there right at the epicenter of the shift, wherever in the world that was, to monitor and lead the new coming into form. Sounds crazy, but…well, I was of pioneering stock, a groundbreaker, a forerunner. Right now LA was it, the epicenter. The next big wave was here, and we were riding it. That was all that mattered. Never mind the old filthy garage with its 50 years of cobwebs hanging from the ceiling.

9

Kundalini Yoga Teacher Training

High on Breathing *Getting Purified and Enlightened *Multidimensional Experiences

Not long after our wedding, I made it to yoga teacher training in Phoenix, Arizona.

I don't know how we did it. There were about 35 - 40 of us living and doing yoga in a small one bedroom house for several months. Well, I do know how we did it, we did it because we were in an altered consciousness the whole time, high, high, higher than any kite, higher than on any drugs and higher! We were in this state because of breathing, breath of fire, continuously, day in and day out. We were cleaning out our minds; we were getting purified and enlightened.

We were very crowded being so many of us in this small house. There were people everywhere, all the time; you couldn't escape them for a moment. The house had only one bedroom and one bathroom, thus there was only one toilet. This meant there was a line (a queue) to get in, all day long. We slept on the floor side by side quite close on our individual bedrolls. I was assigned a small section of the bedroom just big enough for my bedroll to stretch out on the floor, and a section of a shelf for my toiletries and clothes.

We were there to do yoga, and that's what we did. We did yoga exercises, breathing and chanting all day and into the night, practically nonstop. We took short breaks, for watermelon, or just water; for simple meals or none. We ate as a group according to how much money or food was available each day; sometimes there was nothing at all. One thing we knew for sure, we were there on that yoga room floor every morning at four am sharp for our "morning Sadhana" (Spiritual Practice). We paid very little for the course; nobody had money and nobody cared.

We were there to do yoga, that's what mattered. Not so much to learn about yoga, but to do it. We had to transform ourselves; to clean out our negative and limited programming from our families and culture. It was so powerful I was convinced this would bring me a life of what I truly wanted, whatever that might be, to be of service, to give all I had to humanity and, of course, to change the world.

One day during a break I went outside into the back yard. I remember that the sky was a beautiful blue, the staircase I was holding onto, a beautiful white. I felt a total separation from myself as I knew myself. I felt I was a fully multidimensional being. My "I" was many selves and each self was also multidimensional, existing in many realities.

No one had specifically addressed that in class. It felt like I was asleep and dreaming and hallucinating and I couldn't "wake up" and get back to "normal" consciousness. Just as in a dream, or on drugs, all kinds of uncontrollable nonsensical thoughts were passing through my head; I felt completely out of my mind. Since everything we were doing was for the purpose of cleaning out the subconscious I assumed that was what was happening. I enjoyed the sense of being free from the control of my conscious mind.

We were on silence most of the time. This was it. Yoga was done with eyes closed. The energy was being gathered within. It was not about getting to know each other. I don't remember anybody there, let alone their names. We rarely talked, probably didn't even introduce ourselves.

One of the exercises was to write about our life without using the word "I"; the purpose was to help "eradicate ego". Individual consciousness and competition with others was a trap. We had to develop group consciousness. Since I would spend the next 18 years following someone else's idea of "ego eradication", I was learning a lot about what other people thought "ego" meant.

It was the energy coursing through my body that I loved. My body was so into it, I became totally addicted to it, I didn't want to stop, ever. It felt so fantastic. I felt that this energy would soon give me the power to do anything. Move mountains, walk on water, heal with miracles, and transform this very world into what? Into a world of love and service, healing and self-empowerment.

I would go to sleep at midnight and wake up after a mere few hours having had sufficient sleep. My body had a life and mind of its own. Waking up in the morning would mean finding my body automatically and joyfully reaching straight up into wheel pose, hips high up, hands and feet holding me up, and hands almost reaching my feet under my bowed body, and staying there with breath of fire. There was no stopping it. It never wanted to stop! My body would continue quite happily breathing away during all these postures, for hours at a time. It was only a thought from the mind saying, "Hey, let's shift position, that'll be more fun," that caused it to shift.

We had been breathing very powerfully for weeks, and one day I found myself not breathing. Not only that, I realized I had not been breathing for a while. By then I knew of yogis who had been buried alive to show that life could continue without breathing, it wasn't just a question of oxygen: if you had accumulated enough energy called prana in your body and your cells, you didn't need normal breathing to stay alive.

So while lying there relaxing between exercises I noticed how full of energy I was. I didn't know how much time had passed that I was not breathing. I simply did not need to; there was so much stored oxygen, life force, prana in me that for a long time, I didn't need to breathe. It was an amazing feeling, but suddenly my mind had a thought, "Hey, wait a minute, you're supposed to breathe and, if you don't, you're supposed to feel fear because you'll die very soon!" So in the moment of suddenly feeling fear, in that moment of constriction, I had to inhale.

Another time after some intense yoga which had gone on for weeks, we were in 'layout' time. Layout was Yoga Nidra, the time at the end of a class when you would lie down and go deep into guided relaxation; go out of your body sometimes, all to harvest the energy. The teacher would play the gong, or sit and sing, or play soft spiritual music.

I was lying on the floor of the sadhana room in deep relaxation, side by side with these 35-40 yoga companions. Everything we did was magnified exponentially by our numbers. I was deep down into the relaxation, in a highly sensitized state. Suddenly out of nowhere came a whooshing, scuffling, scuttling sound and something dropped down hard on my chest and belly. I felt the pressure and weight of animal paws and heard panting in my ears. The impact was such a shock that it was like a part of me separated from me, as if a part of my consciousness leapt out of my body.

I found myself - though I was no longer a Self as such - I was an uncontained, floating part of a vast pure limitless consciousness field, just being, floating, full of deep awareness and wonder, here and somewhere, and everywhere. I was in an unlimited space, wondrously open and free, wild and expanded. There were no dimensions, no measurements, no beginning, and no end.

The city and the desert and the mountains were far away way down there beneath me, I had a sense of the whole of the city of Phoenix beneath me, yet I was not "I". I was looking down on the city, I was everywhere, I was not limited by a form or any mode of getting around, I simply was everywhere, part of it all, one with it all. I felt completely free, being able to see everywhere without eyes and body, just enjoying myself and marveling at it all. At the same time, I had full regular consciousness and self-will, to go here or there, to fly freely like a bird anywhere.

It was so much fun! Why should it stop, I could and would do this forever! There was no need to return to my body. Eventually somebody noticed my body was lying there motionless long after class was over and informed the teacher. He became concerned that I was not responding to his questions and he and the others started trying to make me sit up. I didn't want to relate. I wasn't interested one little bit. I was in a wonderful other world, I loved this world, - don't take me out of it.

For some days afterwards I didn't want to hear or speak or relate to anybody, didn't want to talk. I simply didn't want to leave this this wondrous, empowered state of joyous oneness in bliss. And it felt like my true state, the "Real Me"; the ordinary world seemed so boring in comparison! I tried to communicate the experience to my teacher, and found words could not do it; it was beyond any possibility of capturing in words. It still is.

Word came that I was to join my new husband who had already moved to San Rafael in California's infamous Marin County. The Yogi was directing our destiny. We obeyed his commands.

10

An Ashram in Trendy Marin County – First Valentine's Day Birth

**Ashram Community Living *Idealism
*Pregnancy, Motherhood, Parenthood and
Responsibilities *Guilt over Parents
Kundalini 'Amrit' Experience

"If humans with full individuality would regain group consciousness, they would have a god-like power to create, alter and shape things on Earth! And humanity is collectively moving toward such a group consciousness of the new kind."

--Russian DNA research

Elandra's Holo-Perception

"A god-like power" — could it be the destiny of the human race to recognize instant healing, telepathy and teleportation and such, as perfectly natural and normal?

Hargobind Sadan Ashram was on a very elegant and gorgeous road in San Rafael that dead-ended up to a mountain. It was a beautifully appointed old mansion with a swimming pool, very large high-ceilinged rooms, upstairs servants' quarters and special second staircase, 6 bathrooms, an enormous elegant entryway. Up to 20 people lived there easily on three floors with multitudes of bedrooms. The spacious living room could hold a party of 100 people, and was in use as the yoga class and sadhana room.

I arrived straight from two months of intense yoga, dressed in white. I had acquired more white outfits having found a sewing machine and managed to sew myself some while I was in Phoenix. Vikram expressed astonishment, "I didn't know you had enough domesticity in you to have ever learned to sew!"

"I didn't know either," I laughed, "No one taught me; I must have just inherited the ability from   watching my mother!" My mother's sewing skills had kept us beautifully dressed as a child even in the lean impoverished stressed years of wartime Europe. Because of our beautiful handmade clothes, when we went out we were treated with deference as if we were rich. She had continued to sew beautiful clothes for me throughout my life at home as a teenager, including the artistically decorated ballroom dresses of hundreds of yards for my dancing competitions.

So I just thought everyone could sew! I was shocked that not everyone was wearing white. I thought, "What's the matter with these people, why be living in an ashram if you aren't wearing white and doing yoga at every possible moment, why this laid back attitude?" I was all gung ho for full enlightenment, which had to be just around the corner. These ashramites were sweet people of good intent and I must have challenged them with my new found fanaticism for yoga!

By now my horrified and shocked family had realized that their only daughter who had the world at her feet was rejecting her life of glamour, riches and splendid opportunities (the kind that almost everybody dreams of as the highest dream you can have!) to live in an ashram together with 20 - 30 would-be yogis, with no real source of income and no apparent interest in getting one.

Hargobind Sadan Ashram - Culloden Park Road, San Rafael, California

As I had come to expect, the consciousness and knowledge about food, health and cooking was impressive. We actually had a professional vegetarian chef living with us, and I threw myself into learning healthy cooking. The kitchen and dining room were also enormous. The kitchen had a large glass built-in wall enclosure which held rows of large preserving jars filled with spices. This really impressed me. These people were serious in their nurturing and nourishment of their bodies, as well as enjoyment of good food.

I was brimming with idealism. This would be a way of life that would bring consciousness to change and help the world. Even as a teenager at University I was appalled at how the world was becoming more and more materialistic with ever more suburbs and more concrete. This would be a way of helping people live more spiritually, and naturally and sustainably.

We learned about group consciousness and really believed we could change everything by getting up at 3am to gather in the 'sadhana room', designated the most important room of the house, for sadhana, spiritual practice, which meant to do yoga, meditate, chant, recite mantras and prayers, and sing Kirtan, divine music in praise of God, devotional sacred singing. We would then become happy and enlightened and attain god-like powers to help everybody and make the world a better place for our children and their future.

We would be freed by the power of the sangat (spiritual family) and group consciousness. I had read, and it had resonated as true, in Yogananda's book and in other books, that you have to learn to obey, hang your ego up on a hook. So I believed in the books, and the guru and everything he said. All we had to do was do what he said to do, so I did it with utmost zeal and conviction, - and joy.

It was a joy to have a purpose in life, a worthwhile direction. I didn't know then that Ashram life would be mostly about hard work and sacrifice. I didn't realize that we would be experiencing the criticism, doubts and fears of the ego in everybody around us including ourselves!

Intentional community has a way of bringing up stuff, severe challenges and we soon learnt that the yoga of relationship is the most difficult and demanding spiritual path of all. If you think relationship with one person is hard, try sharing a kitchen with up to 30 people, even a great big one! Oh my, but we learned so much, and I loved learning.

It was a little like being married to so many people, and the enormous benefit we acquired that has stood us in good stead to this day is that our understanding of and discernment about people was greatly enhanced. We were on a roll, and I wanted to be a part of this wave. I truly believed there was nothing we couldn't accomplish in group consciousness.

I loved the transformational energy of the times, especially in the Bay Area north of San Francisco. The USA was so big, everything was so big! Denmark, New Zealand, and England they were tiny in comparison! So huge, the country itself, and the thinking! And the cups, plates, glasses, the food servings, the pancakes, the stores, the cars, the roads, the houses and 31 flavors of ice cream!

I loved Americans and California. I loved suddenly having a big family of friends. Antion was well known, respected and looked up to, and he was a genius, the first to master the complex music and the language of our new life.

I started teaching yoga classes. All kinds of extraordinary characters were attracted to the yogic ashram lifestyle. The Bay Area Berkley culture was teeming with counter culture types, so our lives were filled with them as they were most keen to show up for classes searching for change, enlightenment, something.

We taught that to get off addictions you had to have something to put in its place. It was the job of Kundalini Yoga to replace the addictions; a basic of the teachings was that drugs and Kundalini yoga were not a wise combination.

We wore long skirts or saris, and so did the yoga students. No yoga tights and fashion statements in those days. We were trying really hard to be spiritual, not sexy; the teachings were that sexy was bad and spiritual was good. And to be spiritual you had to look spiritual. That meant pure white shapeless loose Indian outfits, with always covered up legs and arms.

One time when I was directing my class into shoulder stand the next thing I knew, there were a pair of bare legs sticking up in the air and as they rose ever higher   fabric was cascading downwards all around like a waterfall, revealing more and more naked hips, buttocks and crotch, till even bare breasts began to show while the voluminous frilly Indian cotton dress was forming a pool on the floor totally hiding her face and shoulders.

Since all the students were upside down they missed this perfect display of naked vaginal anatomy, and would not have batted an eye anyway. Even as I was trying to be nonchalant and ignore this unexpected full body nudity, I decided to forgo the next exercise of the kriya, which was scissoring the legs wide apart.

This display from the freedom loving 60s and early 70s were typical examples of the earnestness of the flower power drive and eco hippy-dom search. Now I understood a little better why we were supposed to wear long pants and long cover up top. It had to do with focus, not rebellion, awareness of one's energy focus, not puritanism, and of conscious and unconscious intent from a place of inner chakra balance, as I was to learn later in my healing work.

The characters that lived in the ashram was truly characters: there was one guy called Billy who was so intent on achieving enlightenment right now that he altered and rebuilt his car especially to cater to the uninterrupted continuity of his yoga practice. One day I was to experience this achievement first hand.

Every morning after sadhana we would have a compulsory group meeting to determine the organization of the day's "karma yoga" the cooking, cleaning or anything else needed. On this day I needed a ride so it was organized that I would be riding with him. As I opened the door of this old limousine, a powerful stench of incense and sage greeted me, along with clouds of smoke. I was astonished to notice through the mystical misty atmosphere of the vehicle's interior the   curtains of spiritual paraphernalia hanging everywhere, beads and malas, decorations with pictures of gurus pasted up and attached in every conceivable space and corner including the roof.

He had taken the front seat out of the car and built a plywood platform to sit on, so that he could sit cross-legged - in full lotus - while driving. He had figured out how to drive, change gears and brake without using his feet. He worked the accelerator with a long stick.

The back seat was normal though, and I climbed into it gratefully, feeling relieved it was still there. I watched, apprehensive but fascinated, while this guy never stopped chanting and running his mala between his fingers of not just one hand but both as he navigated this jalopy through the streets of the elegant yuppiedom that was San Rafael and Mill Valley. Feeling like my life was not in my hands I prayed for safe deliverance to my destination.

As with many of us ashramites and would-be yogis, any ordinary conversation was beneath him, a waste of time. It just wasn't what he was here for, it was not his destiny. He rarely spoke, just chanted continuously all day and night. He did not want to miss a single second of Om Namo Shivaya, Om Mani Padme Hum and Sat Nam, which three mantras he alternated continuously.

Ashram life was rich with visiting teachers or dignitaries we hosted and served. The Yogi befriended various teachers and would send them to the ashrams to share their expertise. We hosted continuous classes and workshops in all manner of related spiritual topics, such as healing, reflexology, nutrition, herbs and massage.

We were always either preparing for receiving guests or going to visit other spiritual centers, and of course, above all, taking these continuous courses from the Yogi for purification of our subconscious. After all, we all had neuroses, which the Yogi called 'interlocking neuroses', and we had to clear them.

I was in good health and couldn't understand why I started feeling sick and nauseous, especially in the morning. When someone suggested I might be pregnant I was shocked, what? Noooo, no way, couldn't be, never thought of such a possibility.

Once again my life was about to be turned around dramatically. But I found myself in the right place at the right time because right there where I lived was the very center of the natural Childbirth revolution in USA. I immediately started reading up on every book I could get hold of.

I had been enthralled with the energy of London and LA. The experience of being unexpectedly pregnant caused me to find myself in yet another power spot here. I was struck with the subtle energy and power of the consciousness, that sense that the best and brightest were here, moving energy to change the world.

Even more so than LA this was the happening place, certainly when it came to consciousness around how to bring a human being into the world in the best way possible. The midwives were supported by an awesome holistic medical doctor and everyone pregnant in the Bay Area was reading the Lamaze and the Bradley method books advocating home birth, it was all the rage. I was thrilled to be receiving the very best of care for my planned home birth.

These were wonderful times of learning and joy which turned out to be also preparation and study for my future career. The Yogi taught that at the time of 'quickening' at 120 days the soul would come in, and this time was to be celebrated with a ceremony. The pregnant woman was to be relieved of work, stress and duties. She was performing a divine function for humanity.

Antion and I studied natural childbirth together and went to childbirth classes and it was there that I felt the first pangs of labor, so that we had to leave class to return home to have the baby. Seven hours later on Valentine's Day early in the morning of February 14th, 1973, on her father's birthday, a beautiful little girl was born. We photographed the whole birth, it was such a miracle, and I felt love for this baby that I could never have imagined possible. We were in wonder seeing her father's long fingers and toes replicated.

That night many of the Ashram members gathered to honor her birth.

Fifteen hours later - February 14th 1973 - celebrating Pritam's birth

I was ecstatic with joy and delight. As I started breastfeeding I noticed a whole new attitude towards my body, it was a sacred giver of life, in no way a sex object, wow, liberating, beautiful.

This was such an amazing experience that I chose childbirth teaching as a profession. I had studied the teachings of the Yogi on the subject, and set about writing it all up for the benefit of others. They included the concept of 40 days of special care for mother and baby by a specially trained woman. As the consciousness spread - in those days no one had heard the word 'doula' - we were the forerunners and our teachings did indeed help support the spread of natural childbirth and postpartum care at home.

I sent pictures to my parents, wanting to reassure them and share my life. My guilt and pressure to visit them was growing. The Yogi said I had to get a 'green card' first, (document needed for legal residence in USA) but this was taking time. I knew that after 2-3 years of constant promising to visit them they feared that I was involved in a brain washing cult.

The pressure was increasing. It was July of 1974 and Vikram was gone in England for a few weeks with our 18 month old daughter. I decided to take things into my own hands; good timing. I would leave for NZ. I arranged for a Sufi friend to take me to the airport and started secretly packing and preparing, hiding my suitcase in the basement.

We had a newly created meditation room upstairs on the top floor which required some special daily rituals. These new spiritual practices involved reading sacred scripture in *Gurmukhi* (the Sanskrit-based language of praise of the Creator), and then bowing down in humility to place forehead to floor. Vikram was the only one who had learned how to do all this correctly according to tradition. Upon his departure I was given the job, the 'seva' (selfless service) of tending to this sacred space while he was gone.

Secrecy was not in my nature, and deceit of any kind was abhorrent to me. My secret plans magnified my inner turmoil, causing my feet to take me to the room frequently for respite from my intensifying inner agony . Fate intervened and gave me my most extraordinary altered consciousness experience of all.

I'm on my knees on the floor, bending forward. My forehead touches the floor, and in that moment of contact, whoosh! body and soul is inundated with an inner imploding of indescribably delicious bliss. A flowing and flooding of sweetness sweeter than all the sweetness in the world! It's pouring through me, through every cell, and it's both physical and beyond physical, and every organ and cell is orgasm-ing. The sweetness is overwhelming, intoxicating, my body and my consciousness filled with ecstatic joy.

I had read in the sacred texts that "by the grace of God" the pineal gland could "turn upside down" to release its nectar called 'amrit'. This must be what's happening!

Even all the Kundalini experiences I had had so far did not prepare me for this. And at this point I had been on a long break even from intense yoga breathing, which was not recommended during pregnancy and breastfeeding.

Actually, nothing could have prepared me for this, and it took me over so completely I simply forgot all thoughts of leaving. I had had many powerful Kundalini experiences, but this was way beyond. This extraordinarily ecstatic state didn't diminish for some three weeks, too late for me to leave.

Our three years in San Rafael were busy not only with responsibilities of pregnancy, childbirth and breastfeeding, but also with our duties traveling as a Kirtan group to sing at numerous places in the Bay Area.

The Bay Area was the happening place at this time of spiritual consciousness explosion. We were involved with many gatherings and celebrations such as Comet Kahoutec and Meeting of the Ways, where spiritual teachers would get together, such as Swami Satchidananda, Ram Dass, Kriyananda, Pir Vilayat Khan, Dr. Mishra, Ajari and many others.

I was delighted when Ram Dass accepted our invitation to come to the Ashram to give a talk, and eager to see him again. It was just one week after Pritam was born, and I was happy to take pictures of him holding her. He was as present and compassionate as in those days when I knew him in London.

Ram Dass holds Pritam - March 1973

11

Return to Southern California – Second Valentine's Day Birth

*Move to Anaheim *Peacefully pregnant*
My Parents Visit and are Freaked
Birth of Siri Lakshmi

In February of 1975 I finally received my green card and so was able to visit my family in NZ. When I returned to California Vikram Singh had moved us to our new home in Anaheim, Orange County, to a small ashram of only one couple.

I was happy sharing my simple daily domestic life with just this one very sweet and kind woman while the men went out to work. At peace in this quiet life I felt immeasurably rich in what mattered to me. I loved this tiny shed in the garden, where Pritam could play safely and I could meditate. Most of all I felt I had a purpose, a destiny, and I was divine, living a divine life.

I was a mother first and foremost, giving my all to it, as best I could with all I had and with all I knew. In my mind we were the divine couple and I was the divine mother pregnant with the divine child. I was on a natural high from the joy of loving my precious daughter, who was so much fun, and the joy of pregnancy and loving my new baby to come.

And then there was my worldwide larger family of we white dressed ones, of like mind and love, whom I would see every Sunday, and together we were modeling a conscious and healthy life for the world to see and live and be saved by.

One day Vikram Singh said to me, "You know, this was the time we conceived Pritam a few years ago. What do you think, should we have another child? They can be company for each other". I reflected, our first daughter had never ever even been "a twinkle in her father's eye", no, not one single thought in my head or his. Our second daughter by contrast was very deliberately wanted and planned.

In our still young and immature barely 30 minds this seemed like a wonderful idea. There were no   thoughts about whether we would make it financially, about the need to save to buy a house, pay for college or retirement. Our ancestors and my parents had all somehow survived and thrived through their transitions and so would we.

My parents came to visit from NZ and I knew they would be horrified to find us living in a shed in the garden, owning neither house nor furniture. I deeply loved my parents who had given me so much and whom I feared I had abandoned. But my need to forge my own life even if it was so totally different from theirs was stronger than my concerns for them.

They were sweet, they didn't say - but I knew they were thinking, "What a loss, our beautiful daughter who was destined for such great things, who had such brilliant accomplishments in all fields, who had won the world championships in dancing, with her beauty and her brains together, ending up pregnant with her second child in a little shed, poor with no money, how sad, what a waste".

They had no idea that inside I felt so infinitely abundant in a way that had nothing to do with money. There were times when cash was short but it didn't matter, we always had what we needed, we lived by vision, not by comparison with others. I was so high from my ideals. I was excited to be changing the world. I believed that we could make a difference by letting go focus on personal materialism and worldly ambition in favor of commitment to a spiritual path. Everything was about the journey to live in super consciousness. We would make it, and everyone would understand this, and the time would come when we would not be considered weird or foolish any more.

The cashier at the local supermarket knew me, and asked one day, "When are you due?" I said, "Tomorrow, Valentine's Day". With utmost certainty. This conviction came from a place inside me I was not even aware of.

I wasn't making a conscious effort to have my second baby on the same day as the first. In fact, I had a few weeks to go in my pregnancy. And at that moment I had no symptoms or signs whatsoever that labor was near. Still, I was well prepared, with a midwife friend spending the night, as well as a doctor friend. That night getting ready for bed I opened all the windows very wide, a decision I was to later regret.

I'm waking up at about 2.00am, coming into awareness of being immersed in a most wonderful dream, that's so divine and glorious I don't want to wake up, and I'm clinging to the memory to luxuriate in it some more!

But I have to. Oh, oh my, something is happening in my body, so powerfully that I have no choice. I just can't believe this, aah, ooh, the birth is happening now, right now! Gasping with the intense unrelenting sensations of pressure and pain, almost unable to talk, I'm shaking my husband, "Wake up! Quick!"

Ooh, the waters are already breaking! Gripped by forces beyond my control, I cannot think, I know nothing; I'm just an instrument, a tool, a birth canal, a baby birthing machine.

Vikram's gone, in the first moments of waking he's rushed out of the room. I'm alone with baby coming fast, trying to slow it down, clenching everything, gasping, panting with the intensity, and trying to speak, to call out, "Come back!"

I'm dimly aware that this must be the part of childbirth called 'transition'; I know this because of my childbirth teacher training with the Bradley method. The head is already passing through the cervix, (the neck of the womb), the part of labor notoriously the most difficult and painful and normally expected to last about 20 minutes - minimum. Naturally, the enormous amount of stretching needs time, and so labor is generally at least 6 -7 hours long.

So how can this be, I've had no labor! And now, oh my, the baby is crowning! It's coming! Suddenly Vikram is there with the midwife, just in time, the head is out now, and now popping out, one arm, next arm, and whoosh! A big plopping sound, whole body, fully born, it's a girl, it's a she!!!

Wonder of wonders. No labor, no difficulty, no problem. She just shot forth into life, making a funny little sound with a cute little smile and captivating look as if to say "Hi everyone, I'm here! Let's have fun, what's next?"

Wow, what a miracle. All in a matter of minutes, - way faster than it took me to write this! Up to the breast to suckle, she knows how to do it. Tremendous joy and excitement. The placenta is born; we're cutting the cord, and finally becoming calm enough to realize that the room is way cold, let's close the windows fast!

After some time nursing this beautiful little girl, I reluctantly relinquish her to her father's hands to be placed into a little basin of water by the bed. We had planned this in line with the latest home birth idea, the "Leboyer method" to return the child to its familiar water environment; and there she lies looking calmly relaxed. No crying whatsoever.

Suddenly commotion and scuffling in the hallway outside, there's Pritam, the birthday girl sister, three years old today, excitedly running into the room. Her mouth breaking into a huge smile, she's eagerly rushing over to greet her new baby sister, she just can't wait to see and touch and hold her. She loves her immediately! What a birthday present for her, a sister! We celebrate three birthdays with ice cream and cake.

The doctor is disappointed having slept through it all. And no pictures of course this time, no camera near, and no time.

Pritam and Siri Lakshmi 1976

So our second daughter Siri Lakshmi was born almost exactly to the hour three years after Pritam. Both born on their father's birthday, Valentine's Day, the day of love. What does that mean? It was a sign...Someone figured out the odds, billions, almost impossible.

She leapt into this world already with a huge energy and personality, and extraordinarily cute and adorable with much smiling and lots of laughter. Later her father was to announce (quite proudly too), "I can either be head of the Ashram or Siri Lakshmi's father, but I can't be both".

12

San Diego Kundalini Yoga Center & Ashram

*Founding The Institute of Prepared Birthing & Mothering *Girls go to School in India *Publishing Yoga books*

After a year in Anaheim and Los Angeles, we moved to San Diego where we would spend some thirteen years as directors of the San Diego Kundalini Yoga Center and Ashram Teacher Training Center.

I established yoga classes, held teacher trainings and started writing yoga manuals partnering with editor/publisher Alice Clagett. My enthusiasm for childbearing translated into becoming a childbirth teacher, midwife and co-creating the *Institute of Prepared Birthing & Mothering* with my midwife for Siri Lakshmi's birth.

Vikram Singh (not yet Antion) and I became respected international teachers, travelling and teaching, raised our two beautiful daughters (schooled in a genius level highest IQ classroom) and ran businesses. Vikram became a plumbing contractor and I threw myself into childbirth teaching and midwifery. We bought a half-finished shell of a house and remodeled it into a beautiful home as part of the Ashram complex of three houses.

We moved into the house before it was finished and spent several years working on it until it was done, investing our own time and money into a project that did not really belong to us. Later we had the opportunity to buy it for its assessed market price from the organization. This transaction created a financial windfall for the Ashram. We designated this money to fund our dream of a school of sacred music Kirtan, and to purchase a more suitable yoga center with more parking.

We kept on working on ourselves: the idea and ideal was to "get rid of the ego". The worst thing we could hear or say about each other was "You are in your ego." And we said it a lot - whenever we didn't like something about another! One tough yoga exercise was called 'ego eradicator'; you had to hold your arms up for a long time. We were determined. We had to be egoless and pure to help others and to save the world!

People would hear about us and come for help. One day we were contacted by some spiritual teachers from Mexico who were terrified and demoralized by what they believe were black magic attacks. They were besieged to the extent that those to whom they had turned for help were being mysteriously attacked; one had his house burnt down, another died mysteriously.

The idea that we could be harmed was laughable to us. By this time I felt confident that, by the power of my dedication, I had built up a spiritual 'bank account' that I could call upon in the event of any need; both for my own use and for the benefit of others. Surely we were invulnerable in the power of spiritual protection from so many years of 3am rising, cold showers, Kundalini yoga and breathing, plus the sheer will power needed to live such intense lives in group consciousness.

I could feel my aura was pure, strong, and powerful and believed this was due to the remarkable and rich tradition of beauty, power and protection which came from Guru Nanak. Our tradition celebrated the divine feminine Shakti in the power of sacred chant and song. We felt protected and spiritually invincible.

We enrolled our girls in the San Diego School District where they were tested and found to be highly gifted. They were moved into a special program to be given the best possible education. I was fortunate to become an employee of the school where they studied, first as media center director and then as a counselor.

On the cliffs of Leucadia, California - 1978

At that point, Ashram living seemed to us to provide a perfect lifestyle in which to bring up children. We were living our lives in dedication to a Higher Power that was directing our lives and making them meaningful. We believed that, if we put our spirituality first in our lives, our children would be most secure. They would grow up strong and fearless and balanced and heroic, able to make similar choices themselves. We taught them to chant the morning prayer of Guru Nanak. They read comics of the Sikh Guru's lives, Divine Beings who had often sacrificed their own lives for the purpose of upholding freedom of belief for others. I was hooked by a lifestyle, spirituality, never looking ahead or imagining that there would be any other path for me.

In spite of my dedication, still there were tests. One day I was in despair, devastation and crying inside over a betrayal by one who had been a friend. My wounded being called for help, and suddenly there he was standing next to me on my left. In his endless compassion, Guru Nanak revealed himself to me in a vision of his physical presence I knew it was him, there was no question.

His white hair and beard looked just as in the painting we had hanging in our sadhana room, only more brilliantly white and shimmering with life. His eyes were surprisingly a brilliant blue and radiating with a divine sweetness and compassion. The amazing thing was that, even though he appeared by my side rather than in front of me, I still could see and feel him so perfectly. His presence was overwhelming, as if my eyes and my seeing were everywhere. Instantly the power of solace and comfort was there, healing my heart and filling me with an inexpressible joy.

For some weeks afterwards my consciousness was in total ecstasy; everything I did, I did in a state of oneness with all things. It was utter bliss, feeling Guru Nanak's total presence. I can remember sitting, brushing my six year old daughter's hair. I felt so full of love, with a sense of exploding inner joy that was almost unbearable. I felt like I was flying inside. It was beyond love, even personal love, it was divine love. I started writing poetry, something I had never done previously.

I felt I was a devoted mother who wanted the best for my little girls. I spent time studying what would constitute the very best kind of education and applying my studies to giving them the best I could. I felt if only I could just have no ego, and turn my "emotions to devotion", they would grow up happy and well adjusted, and able to find themselves and their true calling. I wanted to give them all that I had not received, nothing else ever occurred to me. Of course I assumed their calling would be to spirituality like mine… not for a moment did I consider that they might not be interested in my version of it!

In spite of our sacrifices and dedication to our spirituality and our children the Yogi would constantly tell us that we were neurotic Americans, inadequate parents, and that our children needed others to take care of them for their optimal growth. It was obvious to us that American culture, with all its advertising focused on sex and violence, was not good for children. We were following his teachings to not have radio and TV in our Ashrams. We were absolutely intent on giving our children the best of everything

At the Yogi's direction, the organization created a boarding school in India for the American children. He wanted us to send all the children to India for the best possible schooling. Even though we were terrified at the idea of them not being with us, we trusted the Yogi and truly believed that this would be the finest education of all, a private expensive boarding school. I myself had always wished to go to a boarding school; my favorite books as a child were boarding school stories. I had wonderful fantasies that this would give our girls a fantastic start in their spiritual and scholastic lives.

In spite of all the reassurances, the parting was horrible. In pictures taken at the airport we are all smiling; inside we were all in great pain, feeling the separation. I was in agony for three weeks afterwards and could scarcely function. I moved around as if I was underwater, I was hugely traumatized.

Of course, our parents were absolutely freaked, more so than ever before.

After a few months, we started to feel that something was not right. We discovered that their letters home were being censored. We brought them back home one year later and told them that they had the choice whether to return to the school or not. Pritam chose to return to India; Siri Lakshmi chose to stay with us - to my great joy. They were both changed and different from their experience. The next year - when Pritam returned - she had changed even more; they were both acting in a rebellious manner.

Their attitudes are mirroring our unspoken ones. What now?

We began to question and investigate our own beliefs; not easy after almost twenty years of dedicating our lives to what seemed a noble cause. What was going on?

Siri Lakshmi and Pritam 1988

Most yogic paths promote leaving the body in meditation, discarding or transcending the physical. The Yogi's Kundalini Yoga was the ultimate in that regard. We were told to "overcome our emotions" and to "turn our emotions into devotion". Yet we were still so full of unhealed and unexpressed feelings and emotions after many years of intense spiritual work and dedication.

Vikram Singh and I were not really able to express what it was we needed. Now, looking back, it was time to find ourselves in the awareness of our bodies and our emotions, not to deny them. I needed healing, emotional healing, a different kind of support.

We had nowhere to turn, no one from whom to seek a neutral opinion. We needed to look outside our group.

Perhaps even without realizing we opened ourselves to what might be next. And it showed up with a massive force.

13

Miracle Healing Experience

*Miracle Bone Healing *Before and After X-Ray Proof *The Unseen World*

"The intuitive mind is a sacred gift and the rational mind is a faithful servant. We have created a society that honors the servant and has forgotten the gift."

-Albert Einstein

"The process of the transformation isn't something that comes from a higher Will, nor a higher consciousness imposing itself on the body; it's the body itself awakening in its cells. It is a freed in the cells themselves, a brand new vibration that sets all disorders aright....we are evolving into the new species..."

--The Mother, Satprem, "The Mind of the Cells or Willed Mutation of Our Species"

Elandra's Holo-Perception

"Death is a clearing house for useless identities". – Glenda Green, Love Without End, Jesus Speaks. I like this; it refers to our attachments to things like body, name, house, car, clothes etc. When we hold or cling to these things and live by them we are living in duality, insecurity, pain and enslavement having forgotten what we really are, Infinite Awareness, Infinite Consciousness. Actually, what's really important is to realize that our conditioned negative attitudes/unconscious beliefs are also attachments that need healing... We are imprisoned in the realms of a mere five known senses and 'little me' when we are really Akal Purkh, the infinite, undying All That Is, All That Has Been and All That Ever Can Be. Healing is needed and healing means becoming your own clearing house.

San Diego is an amazing city. Located right on the Pacific Ocean and at the border of Mexico, it is also within easy reach of rugged mountains and deserts. We often felt the call to get away from our Yoga Center Ashram responsibilities and head for the hills, to the magic of the desert.

I have always loved nature, from my beginnings in Denmark talking to the birds and plants. From an early age I used every opportunity to test myself to the limits within its offered gravity and adventures. As a tiny two-year-old on my first two-wheeler I would take off downhill at high speed and to the utter consternation of my parents, wildly toss my arms and legs out in the air, screaming with joy, oblivious to the consequences.

On that day in 1991 we had climbed the mountain in Anza Borrego State Park up to the waterfall at the top, and were on our way back down.

I threw myself down that mountain, feeling a wild joyful exhilaration that took me over and drew me on, faster and ever faster, bounding like a mountain goat down that path, racing, leaping and flying over great rocks rejoicing in my sense of magnificent invincibility.

Suddenly I am in another reality. There is no place, time or space as I know it. I am in an all-encompassing present, flying like a bird - only much more open and expanded! An extraordinary thing is happening…time and everything is slowed down, everything in slow motion. I am finding myself in what feels like a parallel dimension, another version of reality. Everything is happening simultaneously, and I am witnessing my body crumpling and dropping to the ground like a stone. I see the body losing consciousness and passing out.

This body is there, my right leg caught between two gigantic rocks, but I am not. I am somewhere else! I am having an amazing, extraordinary and glorious experience. I feel myself being held in the arms of angels, and it's a familiar love, like they are all my dearest friends. Wow, I am here with my beloveds in bliss, in joy. They're all around me, and the atmosphere is magnificent; so many, in a field of high frequency color and sound. Oh my! I feel so loved, so cared for, even revered and adored! It is so beautiful…I am in indescribable bliss, absolute ecstasy. I am here! And I want it to last forever.

My physical body that had fainted now comes to, finding itself becoming aware of excruciating pain somewhere. Yet simultaneously my awareness is detached. It doesn't bother me, as if it is not really me, not my pain. I feel calm, no thoughts, no concerns, everything still in slow motion. Antion hoists me onto his back, and I ride piggy back down the remainder of the long journey to the bottom of the mountain, my dangling foot becoming more and more swollen, more painful until I am lifted into the car, almost passing out from the pain.

On the hour long journey back to San Diego, every little jolt hurt. I was too much in shock to consciously remember the experience with the angels, yet in hindsight, I believe the beauty, sweetness and light of it stayed with me and helped shape what was to come.

After the x-rays are taken, they proceeded to inform me, "The x-rays show your right ankle bones are severely broken, it is imperative you have surgery immediately, you must be at the hospital by 6.30am for your operation tomorrow."

"Is there no alternative?"

"Your foot will be permanently deformed if we do not operate immediately to insert pins through it."

At home I am lying collapsed and exhausted on the bed. As I am lying there, yet another extraordinary experience is taking place. I feel a hand on my foot. But there's nobody in the room. Then I hear a question being asked, from out of nowhere it comes, a voice is saying, "Will you allow this?" I know right away what is meant...I start remembering the many stories of miracle healings performed by holy figures throughout history. So I answer, "Yes."

Immediately I glimpse in my peripheral vision, up on my left towards the window, a shimmery, ethereal energy field ... of angels? All a heavenly effervescent pink, purple, white, gold and blue. Although I do not "see" them clearly, I do notice that they look like the pictures and drawings of angels we are all used to seeing. A part of me is in total wonder, another part unthinking, still numb with shock.

And strangely, somehow it all seems so right, so wonderfully natural and normal! In my mind there is no doubt, and no questions. The pain is diminishing, the swelling going down, my consciousness becoming sweet, light and blissful as I drop gratefully into deep sleep.

Later my chiropractor friend Dr. Wendy (who had been at medical school specializing in radiology and dropped out at the last minute in favor of natural medicine) called to tell me, "I've seen the x-rays. It looks bad. You'll have to have this operation." I started to stammer, trying but unable to find words to tell her about my experience of feeling a hand on my foot when there was nobody in the room, but she broke in quickly, "Don't worry, you're just scared. I'll come over tonight to reassure you."

I was scared alright, not only for my very active future as a yogi, yoga teacher, dancer, runner, hiker, but also very scared of the cost of this operation, which is in my mind (having no insurance) a fortune!

When she arrived, she placed her hands on the foot and with both thumbs gently massaged the bones back into place. Immediately the swelling and pain lessened. I went into an altered state, a relaxed and open very dreamy space. The shattered ankle bones had dropped down into my foot as I was being carried, with legs dangling, down the mountain. So the bones were out of place all over. I felt like she was moving them back to where they belonged! Something seemed to be pulling all the fragments of bone back into place. There was a sensation of bones knitting back together.

Later, in what became my continuous search for explanation, I learned that the body has and is immersed in a "field," an electromagnetic, morphogenetic, etheric field. This field holds the exact blueprint for the physical foot, so that when a healer taps into or hooks up with the field, the energy is catalyzed in the physical cells, bones and tissues to bring themselves back into their original position, manifesting a "miracle healing." It is by virtue of this field that amputated limbs continue to be a source of sensation called "phantom pain" and transplanted hearts are still carrying the thoughts and memories of their owners.

Little did I know at the time that this experience was the next step in my journey to consciousness - that I was being opened and called to my next profession, as a healer destined to learn to catalyze miracle healings for others. Later I learned that bone healing is a specialty of the traditional Kahuna healers of Hawaii.

Suddenly, with a totally uncharacteristic sense of conviction and authority from who knows where, these words exited my mouth, "That's it! My ankle is healed!" I just knew it was healed. Once more, with no question, no doubt, I accepted it. I didn't need anybody to tell me, I just knew it was true. Amazingly I got up off the bed and actually walked on it. Up and down the hallway! It felt totally different. Then, with that same highly unusual decisiveness, I picked up the phone, saying, "Cancel that operation. That's it, I'm not coming."

Strangely, in the morning I knew I had to go back to the hospital and request more x-rays. I have since asked myself, why? Was it to prove it to myself or somebody else? And how could I find the energy to do this since I was in such huge shock and exhaustion? What did I need to learn here…? Did those unseen forces give me something…even more than a miraculous ankle healing?

Back at the hospital, new x-rays taken, we viewed them together. Nobody spoke. We were looking at proof of a miracle, of the impossible! The medical doctor was staring at two sets of x-rays. The one just taken showed my right ankle repaired, bones replaced, glued back where they belonged, in fact, knitted back and fully healed! The other x-ray, taken 24 hours earlier, showed my ankle badly shattered and diagnosed as needing an immediate operation to install numerous metal pins.

The doctor stood there, as if frozen. He was forced to acknowledge that there was no need for the costly operation which he had prescribed the day before, without which I would be "badly deformed for the rest of my life."

The new x-rays proved my ankle was perfectly healed!

Suddenly he was gone, disappeared, no word. Alone, I hobbled out of the room on my crutches. Had I become invisible to them? It was as if I was in a different reality! No one spoke to me; neither the nurse nor the receptionist as I passed by, nobody spoke even a word of goodbye.

In the ensuing weeks, I took time to reflect on all this, thinking:

"Wow! I stood there with proof in my hand of a miracle, of the impossible. Science wants proof. Here it is - x-rays! The medical doctor saw both sets of x-rays. Before and after. The proof was rejected. What kind of science is it to reject scientific proof?"

My ankle bones were completely healed, end of story. He left the room and I never saw him again. They had no further use for me so they ignored me, and so I had become unseen. I did not fit into his reality so his solution was to deny mine!

I had proof, but I did not need proof! I felt I was a living proof, that this world has several dimensions and paradigms of reality depending on perception and belief. I had just experienced up close and for real the dichotomy of two worlds! The current outdated medical paradigm of classical, mechanical, Newtonian worldview thinking, "Your body is a machine, we are the experts who will fix or replace the parts of the machine breaking down, you have no power, no authority, nothing to say or do of value about your body's health and healing, and we have no interest."

I had an incredible story of healing transformation and I had to tell my story, but no one wanted to know. I tried to tell my parents. My mother scoffed and accused me of lying. Friends, their eyes glazing over, quickly changed the subject.

I threw myself into a quest to figure out why. Even though Einstein wrote his theory of relativity in 1905 and in spite of his saying that he "did not come by the laws of the universe by the power of my rational mind," our culture's collective consciousness and consensus reality still operates from this outdated paradigm! It was dawning on me that humanity's resistance to change - even in the face of our highly valued scientific proof! - Still holds us in thrall, imprisoned… in what is a lethal grip of authoritarian dominance. Where did this fear-based reality come from? I had to know and make known, I was drawn on a journey to discover the reality of it.

I said, "Okay, Higher Power, God, I have to know, you have to show me. What is this? Is it some flash in the pan one time only woo woo stuff? (I didn't want to tell anyone about the angels). What kind of consciousness can cause bones to heal instantly? Hey, never mind about the bones and even the extraordinary healing, what about the consciousness that caused it? That's what I'm after!"

Determinedly seeking the keys to miracle healing, little did I know what I was embarking upon, and how my whole life would be turned upside down and inside out.

Afterwards I asked Dr. Wendy how she did it. She said, "I didn't, you did. You're always your own healer. Come and work with me at my Clinic."

14

"Come Work with Me and Be a Healer" – Meeting Louise Hay

*Come Work with Me *New Career as Healer
*Louise Hay: "Elandra, You are Powerful"
*11:11 Solara Activation *The Three Keys to
Healing *Sister Sarita and Don Miguel Ruiz*

I promptly became massage therapist/physical therapist/healer at The San Diego Stress Relief Clinic. I enrolled in massage school and threw myself into taking every single course on healing in southern California, all of which amounted to multitudes of courses and classes in healing.

Dr. Wendy's Clinic was unusual in that there was no listing in the phone directory. It was a healing center which operated purely by word of mouth, and we were always fully booked.

Just walking through the door was an experience, perhaps a healing in itself! You would most often be greeted by a party atmosphere with uproarious laughter, the chiropractor appearing in some new joke outfit, such as a plastic penis nose with balloons attached, there was no knowing what she would do next. She was Wendy to all, everybody loved her and being there was so magical, entrancing, and fun that nobody cared if they had to wait for an hour or two or many more, which they often did. Not only that, they didn't want to leave after their treatment!

Dr. Wendy had designated several rooms for preparing the patients for their treatment with her. One of my tasks was to greet the patient and welcome them into a lovely darkened room for a meditative experience, which involved guiding them to lie down on their backs on a spinalator, -a machine which would deliver a full back massage. They would be fitted with an aromatherapy eye pad, earphones, and left there with relaxing music in what was like a beautiful decompression chamber.

Next I would lead them to another room where I would give them some form of healing work of the many modalities I had been learning. This could be one of many, such as Therapeutic Touch, Pranic Healing, Chakra chelation, Reiki, or Cranial sacral or a combination.

Finally they would be ready to proceed to her treatment room. Occasionally she would call me in to join her to work on them, and mentor me while we watched their aura, chakras and colors changing.

Miraculous healings occurred on a regular basis, diagnosed brain tumors and cancers disappeared. I was trying to figure out how it happened – how our patients' whole lives, jobs, relationships and all would be transformed along with the disappeared brain tumor or whatever. People left there as totally transformed beings, with new lives. No wonder the patients would find every reason to stay as long as they could, and enjoy making friends with each other there in the waiting room.

Louise Hay was one of our patients. She was already famous as one of the earliest who had creatively documented the correlation between physical ailments and emotions, using a revolutionary view of mind/body healing with a chart showing how to empower yourself with specific affirmations. And we had a past in common; she had also been a beautiful model who had chosen a healing spiritual path.

When she would come to the clinic I was somewhat in awe of her, feeling honored to be getting to know the world renowned author/healer. I was nervous in those days, feeling I didn't know enough, - which of course was a gift too that kept me open and learning until the day came when I heard the voice saying "Elandra, give up your need to know."

One day she brought a gift for me. It was her new book, *You Can Heal Your Life*, autographed with a message for me. I opened it and read, "Elandra, you are powerful."

With Louise Hay 1992

This gift was actually a very great gift. It made me aware of how much I did not feel "powerful", which then set me on a journey to understand why. At the time my response was, "Powerful? No way"! It did not compute as true; I didn't feel "powerful"!

Even though I had walked away from my movie star career, and had just spent 16 devoted white-garbed years getting up at 3.30 am to chant and meditate and teach yoga every day, to run a Yoga Center, Ashram, Ministry, and Childbirth-Midwifery-Parenting teaching center, who was I to be "powerful"?

In my mind I was a seeker. I had too much to learn, always looking for more, always never enough. I was still trying really hard to be spiritual and pure and good enough. Throughout school my teachers called me 'self-effacing', in spite of being top of the class with multitudes of honors. Thus I dismissed her compliment…yet I carried it somewhere in my being where it has lived and supported me ever since.

The larger-than-life Dr. Wendy was highly psychic and extraordinary things were always happening around her. We were a unique community and held gatherings and parties for special events. We celebrated the Harmonic Convergence in 1987 at the clinic.

One day she declared that I would soon be leading a huge gathering in San Diego. Patients had been coming in with a book called *Starborne: A Remembrance for the Awakened Ones*, by Solara, and somehow this book and its energy were catalyzing us all toward something that was happening almost spontaneously.

I knew my spiritual energy was high and powerful due to all the years of discipline, but I had no conscious idea of what that meant, how to harness it, what I was supposed to be doing. I decided - as I was learning to do and would do many times - to just go with what I felt led to do from within.

I was learning that in these realms there's no way to figure out it ahead of time, you just have to allow letting go, to 'go with the flow'. It was an inner understanding. But it was hard to accept, that there would be no one to run it by, no one to give approval, that basically these multidimensional insights were not discussable! I was on my own with only my unpredictable and unconscious inner guidance.

Thus it happened that on Jan 11th, 1992, in Balboa Park, about 350 white garbed people stood in a circle so big you could hardly see the other side. Where did all those people come from? Since there was no advertising… all word of mouth?

It was part of a time synchronized worldwide event happening in many countries for the 11:11 activation. There I was, unerringly, calmly and confidently leading them into an enormous spiral. We danced the "wheels within wheels" - as if we had done it before!

What was most extraordinary of all was how it all fell into place with no effort, and practically no planning. There was no advertising, no press, no cameras, and no pictures - as far as I know - of this remarkable event.

The Clinic: with Dr. Wendy and Jennifer (receptionist) - 1992

Another surprising factor was that at this point in my life I was in withdrawal from my 18 year stint of wearing white almost 24/7. I had introduced pastels to my clinic wardrobe, and was feeling an aversion to wearing white, especially for this event, where it was asked of us. In a rebellious mindset I decided I really wanted to wear black and resolved I would! In spite of that decision and desire, the controlling forces of my inner guidance brought my feet straight to the store with the longest racks of white clothes. Perhaps the same experience was had by the hundreds of people (unknown to me personally) present on that day, because every last one of them was dressed in pure white!

In these years and especially these months we, Vikram and I felt we were living in multidimensional realities. It was all so extraordinary I secretly had the feeling we were on a spaceship, and that the doctor was an ET from outer space, -and I loved every moment!

She had hinted at UFO experiences, and spoken of her relationship to Kahuna energy. Something had happened to her in Hawaii. There is a Hawaiian tradition of bone healing - although as far as I know there is nobody, no miracle-working Kahuna with any ability to heal broken bones like mine were healed. Was it Kahuna energy coming through her that created my miracle healing of my shattered ankle?

What is a Kahuna anyway? While the word basically means 'expert', or keeper of the secret, the sense of it refers to one who has developed mastery in some field, has a special gift, or power, or extraordinary abilities, can connect like a shaman with other worlds, and understands the secrets of the paranormal.

One day she said, "I am taking you to lunch to tell you the secret".

My informal apprenticeship with her, my mentor, the doctor, (miracle healer, chiropractor, Kahuna bone healer), was teaching me some valuable principles of healing. Mind you, they were not spelled out for me at the time. It's only in retrospect that I recognize how I learned to believe them, practice and eventually embody and live them as my reality. Certainly at the time, little did I know that I was in training to later become a healer also able to facilitate 'miracle' healings and to work to teach others to do the same.

The first two I identified and started teaching: All healing is Self-healing, and Doubt is the Enemy.

The third was to be told to me on this day, and imparted to me in a most dramatic memorable way. I admired and looked up to her for her amazing work and abilities. I loved working with her, and knew this was something very special she was going to tell me. This would be a very special day. At lunch, over the soup, suddenly she leaned close, "Come here," she said, "Move closer. Lean forward. I'm now going to tell you the secret."

She brought her face very close to mine, and face to face looking in my eyes, smiling big, eyes sparkling, she whispered conspiratorially, "Love is the key."

I was fascinated and continued asking how such healing is possible and why this is not recognized by our medical systems of healing. The Unseen World and the Seen World are diametrically opposed, I mused, in deep reflection on everything I had experienced. Why is this? There are testimonials to such "miracle" healings, I thought, but how can we learn about this, how can I do this too for myself and others? Is it done through technique, is it explainable? Is it a fluke, or can it be taught? Is this about the other 90% of the brain or DNA they say is unused? And what is this 'love'? We have heard that the body has its own self-healing system, but how come it doesn't always seem to work? It's like it has forgotten, or believes it doesn't know!

So, I speculated, how can we all create miracle healing? What if there was not only a predictable way to create such results, but also to maintain health! What if it were possible for me, you, and all humanity to live in a body secure and free from all the ills it is subject to? What if the body itself knows how to do this?

What if there is a place, an actual address within the body where we can uncover that knowing and activate it for permanent healing, health maintenance and ageless living...Michelangelo as he sculpted tells us how the stone spoke to him, so that he could "Cut away all that is not IT." What if the body could speak and tell us how to let go all that is not it!

Will then your body with its own blueprint resurrect itself to its original state, and kuleana, divine destiny? I knew I had to learn how this could happen and how to do this for others. Where was this other paradigm? In the looking I found it looking for me, yes, calling me...

I don't remember how I came to be there that night, at a Center for Toltec-Nagual shamanism, sitting amongst this roomful of people feeling a powerful vortex of rarified energy developing. It was a heady light-headed feeling of coming into and being in touch with other dimensions and worlds... by then not new to me.

What was new was feeling this energy unexpectedly being conjured up by the passionate prayers to Jesus (spoken in Spanish) of a little old Mexican lady - who looked to be about 90. I had had many extraordinary experiences in my years of Kundalini yoga, spirituality and healing, but this was different yet again, and right away I knew this was the real thing.

The woman was Sister Sarita, a healer from Mexico known as a psychic surgeon specializing in heart transplants. She told us, her words being translated, that she was being invited to speak at Heart Transplant conferences, that she had this ability to put in "a new heart" for somebody whose doctor diagnosed the need, and that afterwards her patients would return to their doctors to be reassessed and pronounced fully cured of all heart problems and no longer needing surgery.

I was intrigued. By then I had gained a lot of experience (in my work with the doctor at the clinic) in healing multitudes of conditions and my insatiable curiosity and love of learning was always eager for more witnessing and explanations of what we call miracles.

Her son was introduced, a Mexican medical doctor with no license to practice in USA. Nobody knew him then, he was later to become famous as the author of *The Four Agreements*, Don Miguel Ruiz.

She informed us we were going to learn how to put in new hearts, she would teach us. We were to find a partner; one person would be the patient, and the other the doctor. She taught us to simulate an actual operation. We were to give the injection, insert the IV, hook up the anesthetic, and open the valve to turn it on. Next we were to take the scalpel in hand, and follow the instructions to open the chest cavity. We would take out the old heart, and in its place install a new one. And so we practiced, each taking our turn. The rarified energy was high the whole time.

I wanted Antion to experience this, so the following week, we arrived together. The Center was in a regular house in Normal Heights, we were about 20 people waiting for Sister Sarita to come out. She appeared with her translator as before, and while the room started its spinning act an interesting thing happened.

She and her translator were acting excited and incredulous, pointing at each person one at a time, lips moving; it looked like they were counting us.

Then she announced, "I have waited three years for this day, three whole years for the day when there would be exactly 21 in my class. There has always been more. Now I can tell my story. At that time I received a message from God, saying:

"I want you to make 21 gold medallions to my specifications, with signs and symbols of God on them, and bury them for 21 days under the earth. Then dig them up and place them in the sun for 21 days. Then put them in your purse and carry them with you all the time to your classes until the day comes when you count exactly 21 people. Present each one with a medallion; we will tell you what to say to each".

This was the day, and she was exultant with relief that she would not have to carry these heavy medallions any longer! One by one, she called us up to the front of the room, and presented the medallion along with a special blessing and message for each person about their calling to be international healer/teachers.

Here was yet another reminder of things we already knew deep inside… We were on "the hero's journey"; big changes were coming up for us, another huge shift, another transformation, the next reinventing of ourselves. Already slowly we had been changing our lives, taking dance classes, learning jitterbug together, going to African dance classes, and "expression sessions", and with the support of our new spiritual social circles were breaking loose with some wonderful parties in our lovely home, all alcohol and drug free, with dancing and drumming.

Our 20th Wedding Anniversary Party 1992

15

The Supreme Ordeal

*Divine Disillusionment *The 'Supreme Ordeal' and the Great Gift *Surviving to Reinvent Ourselves *Spiritual Independence *Total Transformation*

"It's by going down into the abyss that we recover the treasures of life".

-- Joseph Campbell

"Few are those who see with their own eyes and feel with their own hearts."

--Albert Einstein

"I do see a new birth of human consciousness underway. And when these things happen they can sometimes happen very fast. So I cannot rule out the possibility that all of us are going to be looking at the mystery and meaning of life in a very different way very soon."

--Graham Hancock

Elandra's Holo-Perception

With regard to group consciousness, there's a narrow line between 'group consciousness' and collectivism. Collectivism is where individuality is subordinated to group consciousness. Had we been too obedient? Had we as a group and individually, quit thinking for ourselves? Had we given up our power and thus lost ourselves? Full individuality in co-creation means self-sovereignty, self-empowerment. Which entails letting go of attachment - to identity, ideas, people, to stuff, and to beliefs. A more enlightened group consciousness remains vigilant, and leaders remain humble so as not to encourage cult consciousness. It's the start to re-membering Who We Really Are.

It looked like I had everything anyone could ask for. I had a spiritual path. I had a man so exceptionally committed and devoted that he was known, admired and revered worldwide for both his spiritual integrity and remarkable musicianship. Our two wonderfully beautiful and brilliant daughters were both in special college level schooling for highly gifted children.

I had a worldwide community of friends, and a sangat. Together with Antion I was leader and head of a Yoga center, a live-in center, ashram, a community, and a congregation. We taught classes in yoga, yoga lifestyle, and all aspects of consciousness and healthy living, including nutrition, spiritual living, health, healing and spiritual relationship.

I had researched and become the author with my partner Alice Clagett of numerous respected manuals on the yoga teachings which are still selling, especially Yoga for Health and Healing. I was running a business, *The*

Institute of Prepared Birthing & Mothering that was so valued in the community and city that even after my partner left town and we disbanded, the demand was such that I continued teaching without advertising for a year.

I had a lovely place to live, in an exclusive pocket of town near the zoo, canyon and a park, an inspiring designer home Antion had created. People would walk in and say, "Wow, this should be in a designer magazine." It was Zen-like white, light and bright, with skylights, creative ceilings, woodwork, and tiling. The bathroom even had two shower heads in the enormous bathtub, a bidet, and skylights. I loved it all.

I loved my new work catalyzing miracle healings at the Stress Relief Clinic of San Diego with the doctor. In becoming a healer, I was learning about being in the body. I learned about goddess energy to honor the body. I studied Taoist internal alchemy, which was hugely profound and practical compared with the yogic obscure texts, which seemed to be about hiding some esoteric secrets for the purpose of holding out the carrot at the end of the stick - to gather students, to retain power? I would study yogic texts and then think, what was that? How is that relevant?

Something was calling me before I knew it. Hawai'i found me in San Diego. I had been studying Hawaiian Lomi Lomi with Mary Golden, the foremost teacher of Aunty Margaret, Hawaii's renowned teacher. I was lying on my own massage table face down, receiving my first Lomi Lomi massage from her. Suddenly I saw a scene in my mind's eye - in full color. We were outdoors in Paradise, surrounded with beautiful vegetation. I knew it was Hawaii, only it wasn't her but a big Hawaiian man working on me!

I knew I was getting a transmission of energy. I had a picture on my sacred space altar of Aunty Margaret and I knew it was she who was connecting with me, initiating me. Years later when I met her for the first time at a Lomi Lomi conference she said something very puzzling to me. She smiled knowingly at me, laughing, and to my great surprise, her first words were, "See how much money you're making?!" as if to say, "See? I showed you your teaching future".

Although to outside eyes everything seemed to be going well on many levels, something else had to happen. I had chosen this, a spiritual path, because I found truth and integrity lacking in the entertainment world. Now what was happening, was it lacking here too? I was at a crossroads.

Deep in my heart, through all these years in the yoga organization I had continued the search for what I already instinctively knew inside, and felt was my destiny in this life, to remember and demonstrate that this world is not the only world, and that it must be possible to bring the polarized worlds together to regain truth and freedom, individually and collectively.

After nearly two decades in the organization, giving my all in service and devotion, my eyes were being opened to see that there was something terribly amiss. I would go to the gym to exercise and instead spend the time in the women's dressing room sobbing my heart out.

Now again, neither yoga nor meditation nor our authority and standing in the organization were going to hold back the inevitable. Long story made short, we recognized it was time for – yet more emotional healing.

We were on a journey, and it had to be a journey to impeccability, to true shamanic values, which does not bypass the unpleasant and the heartbreaking. All is included. All must come to light. I was being faced with the choice to decide, what really matters? I figured it out again and chose again.

We received a call from headquarters that the Yogi wanted the money, the money we had set aside to fund our dreams and plans for the future of the Ashram. He didn't want to talk to us, he wanted the money, he wanted it "now", he would take it, and he did. He had the power. We had to face up to the fact that we were now part of an organization where the leader held all the power and authority with no checks and balances. You don't question. It had become a cult; to question a cult or to leave a cult can be dangerous.

We heard later that our 13 year investment of blood, sweat and tears in the Ashram's future was used to buy political power for the Yogi, contributing towards the election of Bill Clinton.

The San Diego Ashram dream was over.

I would rather be dead than choose something less than total commitment to integrity. All that really matters is the truth, the choice, and my own relationship to truth, within myself. My own integrity. My own values.

I was thoroughly burnt out after years of being at the beck and call of everyone, as a follower, people-pleaser and mediator. It was hard for me to set healthy boundaries and express my truth. I had been looking - longingly - at a magazine called Real Goods Magazine. The cover depicted natural living, a yurt with a river nearby, palm trees, idyllic…Be careful what you wish for - shortly thereafter there we were, living in Hawai'i in a yurt, a river nearby, palm trees...

It was severe recession time in San Diego; we sold our beautiful home at great loss.

So we were as suddenly and unexpectedly uprooted and separated from our whole lives and identities, home, career and community as we had previously experienced several times. We gave away all, and left behind family, community and the organization we had given our lives to for almost twenty years.

And once again family and friends lamented, thinking, "What's the matter with you, what a waste, if only you were normal, you threw it all away again!"

All this was a test of major proportions from the "hero's journey" perspective: the "worthy opponent", the "supreme ordeal," was upon us. After all, we are making a good story here. This is life. This is my life - a story. How we recover and reinvent ourselves is part of the story. And that is the reward and the gift - the transformation.

16

"Home" to Hawaii

*Listening to and Talking to a Tree *Sacred Voices of the Earth *Ancient Timeless Wisdom *Indigenous Mind *Aloha Healing *Chi Nei Tsang*

"The fundamental need of our time, the precondition of creating a peaceful and sustainable world, is the spread of a new and more evolutionarily adaptive consciousness—the quantum consciousness of oneness and belonging."

--Ervin Laszlo

Elandra's Holo-Perception

Already a long time ago, Albert Einstein wrote, "All our lauded technological progress - our very civilization - is like the axe in the hand of the pathological criminal." He goes on to say, "More and more I come to value charity and love of one's fellow being above everything else." It's hard to imagine isn't it, that once upon a time, peace was possible and it was valued and natural. But it was and shall be again... when you remember... Who You Really Are.

We landed shipwrecked on a shipwrecked island! Kaua'i was in shock after the great hurricane Iniki destroyed the whole island. With so many houses blown away there was nowhere to live. We knew no one. A lot of the population had left; both the island and its people were devastated and traumatized. We found ourselves living like shipwrecked Robinson Crusoe in a tent in the rural wilderness of Hawai'i.

We had brought with us two daughters, three cars, and two suitcases. Actually we had landed in Maui intending to purchase property and settle there, where we had friends, but suddenly we were catapulted over to Kaua'i. Our daughters soon organized their lives to return to California. Our families as usual thought we were crazy - even if they didn't say so.

Strangely it was all thrilling for me. The island felt cleansed, momentarily cleared of all the development and relentless materialistic growth.

I was a pioneer again. Like my parents! I remembered Dad's drawing, his dream way back in cold dark war-torn Europe, of a tropical paradise. As it turned out New Zealand wasn't quite that – perhaps compared to freezing Denmark it was – but just a bit cold for bananas and hula girls in grass skirts to flourish! I must have made it to Hawai'i to live his dream as well as mine.

In spite of the devastation I found myself obliviously, madly happy! This was an adventure, like living in a fairy tale! Surrounded with mountains, land, coconut trees, a river, banana trees, palms, tropical warmth, ocean nearby, this was paradise found.

And I was in love - with the Earth! I didn't need anything but this, the *aina*, the sacred Earth. I wanted the Earth, this reality, more than anything, and as little between me and it as possible. It was all that mattered, my love for this sacred land. We had the opportunity to take an apartment, but I wanted my body close to the land. No big house and fancy bed between me and my land, my beloved. It didn't matter that there were plenty of cockroaches, centipedes, mice, huge spiders, rats, feral cats and wild chickens and pigs all around.

I felt like Eve returning to Paradise. I had had a dream a year before; I was Eve putting the apple back on the tree. That meant reversing the story of getting kicked out of the Garden of Eden. Then I realized, as some cultures know, we had never been kicked out; it was not even true! It was a bad dream and a big lie!

The Church, the Christian missionaries of our Western culture made it up way back to control us. The whole of Western culture is touched by this belief – held subconsciously - that we are bad. We are sinners. Whether we are believers or atheists make no difference, it's the Zeitgeist, the inescapable collective belief in our very DNA. No wonder we struggle with feelings of worthlessness and being unwanted.

The enchantment of Hawaii is such that just visiting might be endangering to one's rational financial life and future. Some of us are so entranced that possibly – well, it's only too possible, never having made a deliberate or reasoned or conscious or rational or wise plan to move to Hawaii - before you know it, there you are, relocated, living there!

We lived in a tent on eight beautiful acres with a stream running through it, and then after six months we bought a yurt, held a yurt raising party with our group of new friends, built a deck, and lived my dream life close to nature for five years.

Soon after moving to Hawaii I was in the local library heading for the healing section (as always) when I had a riveting experience. A book seemed to leap down off the shelf at me, opening to these words: "The world will turn to Hawaii as they search for world peace, because Hawaii has the key, and that key is Aloha." Enthralled, I read the Aloha chant about living as one, at home inside, in peace, humility, unity, kindness, acceptance and oneness.

Yurt Raising Party - November 1992

Feeling that Pilahi Paki was giving me a personal message, "Elandra, this chant is for you to learn and use," I took it as such and promptly learned how to chant it, and years later continue to do so with great joy.

Akahai e Na Hawaii   O Hawai'i be gentle

Lokahi a ku like   Stand together in unity

Olu'olu ka mana'o   Let your mind rest in comfort

Ha'aha'a a o kou kulana   Let your attitude be humble

Ahonui a lanakila, Aloha e   Endure and be victorious, Aloha

I set out to find out more about Pilahi Paki, asking everyone I met, including Hawaiians, and was astonished that nobody – or so it seemed at that time - knew anything.

I learned that her Aloha chant was accepted by the Hawaiian legislature in 1983, and that "the Aloha Spirit" was added to the Hawaiian State Charter establishing Aloha as "the working philosophy of Hawaii."

I thought, wow, where else in the world - in the history of jurisprudence – is Love as such accepted as a guide for government and law? Amazing, even secular government recognizes that Hawaii is Aloha, is Love!

Surrounded with the vast immensity of oceans the Hawaiian Islands are some 2,500 miles from any land mass. Home to the largest crystal, some of the highest mountains in the world, and the tallest undersea mountain, the islands of Hawaii are circled by limitless blueness of sea and sky, and graced with innumerable sparkling waterfalls and endless sun drenched beaches. The sheer beauty arouses deep feelings, ancient longings, initiation deep in the soul, back to the dreamed of paradise, the Garden of Eden.

Our Yurt after 5 Years

What is this feeling, this Aloha? You define it for yourself! For me and for so many, it's a calling to your soul's love! It draws you inexorably as if by the Pied Piper, irresistibly, onwards, and inwards, into the melodious sweet and joyful music, sounds of the soul - for the soul.

And into the adoring feeling, of Divine Feminine, The Goddess, She with a capital, She whose energy is synonymous with the forces of nurturing Nature, - along with the grounding supportive energy of Mother Earth.

And the aromas of the aina, - land held sacred, honored and cherished -, the extraordinary loveliness of the tropical flower leis, the whispering fragrances, the heavenly air, the elements of nature, the exquisite ferns, the power of the rain, rivers, ocean and mountains - all with names resonating mysticism, attraction, mystery, all luring us on, all whispering intoxicatingly, "Come, come, give up everything, come to me, we love you, and you know, my love, that love is all that matters!"

And then even more, it's the language! The *kaona* – the hidden meanings, the levels and layers of meaning within the language, that's it, it's the language of soul! Hearing these soul awakening chants, in a language mysterious and exotic, a language just for loving and honoring the Creator, and the Earth, the Creation!

Most of all to me, it's a calling to Home Within, Hawai'i, the very word is a calling home. That means right here, right now in your body. Right now through your seven sacred chakras corresponding to the seven sacred islands… You might even feel the radiant feelings of love, in your body's cells, and then feeling immersed in love, honoring and safety, there you are, evoking dreams, long lost precious feelings, radiating sensations of a wholeness of being, a fullness of fulfillment, a dreaming of an infinitely ecstatic intimacy of beingness. Feeling the inexplicable and enigmatic and ineffable sweetness of everything!

Antion with friend Penny (standing) and Auntie Angeline

Ha means breath and *wai* means water, so *ha-wai* is the very substance of your body, and you are remembering this. And the call to this mysterious "within" will not let you go. It's an ongoing call to embody love; it's cellular healing, and the feeling is, that in the presence of this energy of Aloha, there can be no discord, disharmony, and no illness. Only purity of perception and thought.

The island, nature itself, was revealing its secrets to me. It taught me to directly connect with – Nature, She Herself. I immersed myself in the ancient teachings of a culture which knows about consciousness, miracle healing and how this happens, about simultaneous worlds, and does not deny the unusual, yet cloaks it from uninitiated view. Just living there is Initiation with a capital, because you do not learn in the way you wish to or expect to, and that can come as a shock.

So what are initiations? Let's just say for the moment that they are experiences that show up in your reality which you would consider accidents or problems if you didn't recognize them as having purpose and meaning. They are sent by your soul (your soul is your developing true self) for the purpose of activating change, perhaps even profound change in your world view. Initiations are practical, authentic, personal learning experiences that cannot be understood by the mere mental cognition called knowledge in our Western system of learning.

The first time I was exposed to an ancient wisdom tradition in practice, my mental thinking paradigm was turned upside down. At the time, I was living in the wilderness for what was to be five years with no bathroom (go where "nature calls"). I washed dishes in the rain. My teachers were the spirits of Nature. Unbeknownst to me at the time I was in training, actively living out my apprenticeship! The trees spoke to me, taught me how to heal, and how to chant. They taught me how to listen within and how to know without knowing how.

Elandra far right with dedicated Hula lovers in Halau Hula Na Lei Kupua O Kaua'i

When I joined a *Hula Halau* (traditional school of spiritual studies, chant, song and sacred dance), on the very first day, I was shaken to my core. The *Kumu Hula*, (teacher), said, "I want you to learn just by hearing, listening, memorizing, so get rid of your note-taking, and recorders." That day, as always, being a lifelong avid intellectual student and researcher, I was well-equipped for the gathering of knowledge with notebooks, tape recorders all ready to go. The shock of hearing they were to be taken away threw me totally. "No, no, no!" came an indignant shrieking from within. "Don't do this to me! This is how I have learned to exist in this world and prove my worth!"

This was deep. It felt like my very identity - that I had worked so hard to develop and identify with - was being threatened, like the rug was being pulled out from under me. Actually, it was even worse, it was like, and I imagine, an experience of drug withdrawal for the addict! I concluded that our culturally learned intellectual mind's way of amassing and accumulating knowledge was the ego's way of mustering more control.

I realized that the true teaching in the oral traditions is a transmission of heart, not of intellectual information, and that in their world consciousness is different. In our Western society 'head' (rational/left brain/ego) has been enthroned as a superior master of all and 'heart' (intuition/body/gut feeling) is a second class servant.

In the indigenous world 'heart' is a natural master and 'head' is happily in service.

The "indigenous mind" of the ancient peoples of the world understood how all things are inter-connected through what they call in Hawaii aka fibers. Quantum science calls it a "field" where everything is within everything else, and so everything is holographic, meaning all one part of each other. For the ancients there was no separation, no intellectual or authoritarian compartmentalization; the true teaching in the oral traditions is through transmission of energy from heart.

I love recognizing that, and feeling we can understand and accept what science is now validating, that through this field we are not separated, but a part of all and therefore can perceive and know whatever we need or want to know. Not only can we know, we can also heal, while manifesting our kuleana', responsibility, destiny, that which our soul guides us towards.

One day, with mind racing, heart beating I stood reading a flyer on the notice board from Gilles Marin, about a workshop in Healing Tao, Master Mantak Chia's Chi Nei Tsang. I wrote down the contact info, feeling this must be it! A map, with which I could navigate my way Home, in my own body. Like the great explorers of old, using the stars and remote viewing to the stars. There at the source I would find the answers, the secrets, the origins of all physical problems, and this human condition could be healed and evolved.

In the workshop I learned that the way Home was indeed within. Inside, not out there. We learned to "open the "wind gates" and there it was - a map through the gates and channels of the body. A map with addresses!

Those negative feelings so often stuffed and repressed actually had origins, an address in the body! Problems weren't "all in the head"!

I raced home and practiced on my husband with amazing results for us both in clearing our emotional states. I loved reminding the organs of their own joy filled jobs of moving stuck energy; lovingly making room for the Large intestine/Lung to reclaim its job of letting go on all levels, and the Small intestine/Heart to digest and integrate together with nurturing mother Earth and Spleen the negative charges. I felt the ease and joy of the body/belly intuition that knows how to empower the Chi flow path to consciousness, without need to figure it out in the head. I experienced the organs as inter-dimensional portals. The cells were the time machine.

Everything is in the body (and the body of the Earth). I was experiencing them as a transmitter, with everything there in each organ and each cell, the perceptions that create beliefs, all there under my touch. Dr Candace Pert in *Molecules of Emotion* says "Your body is your subconscious, your subconscious your body." The Mother (of Sri Aurobindo's Ashram in India) said, "Salvation is in the cells." And when I heard the voice of science - Dr Bruce Lipton of *Biology of Belief* - say "Our bodies and our digital technology share the same definition, they are semiconductors with gates and channels"- I knew that was it.

Since birth a part of me has known (at that time an unconscious knowing) that all knowledge is accessible, we are all connected and all is known. I sought a word and a place for it, and found it in Hawai'i - the word itself means "home".

From the ancient ways, called *Hava'iki*, a word, a memory, a place, an energy, spanning continents and the many islands within Polynesia, New Zealand to Hawaii, to beyond, we knew, we sailed, we navigated back and forth, and in our soul and DNA there is a deep knowingness of our original home.

I say "we" because I have experienced memories of this, so I know, where we were. We feel other dimensions of reality, we feel what may be the ancient Homeland called Lemuria, and Hava'iki as known throughout the Polynesian islands. You feel the etheric reality, the sacred islands in a parallel reality. A multidimensional and holographic knowing of their presence through all your senses, and the senses, - not just five or six, but hundreds being opened up to it!

And then, that enables an original natural ability, a super communication known as hyper communication. A communing, soul to soul; a direct, real, authentic communication with the land and trees, so you may hear them speak to you! The tropical vegetation and flowers are alive with messages for you, waiting for you to receive them.

So Aloha is not about philosophy, morals, ethics, religion, faith, or laws. Or what anybody says it is, including me. It's a personal thing. Aloha increases, grows, empowers through feeling it and feeling it by passing it on. How? With every smile, every thought of caring for another, every moment of selfless serving; with the love, kindness, sweetness, and humble-ness you become deeply immersed into the reality of this inexpressible energy. And when you cultivate it till you have it, feel it and know it, nobody can take it from you. Not ever, because this energy is then pure, undying and immortal.

It was becoming embodied in me, becoming real. You can't fake it, because Aloha also means 'to face into, be with.' Face what? The truth. The word calls for your God given ability to discern and to know and to test what is truth – both cosmic universal truth and personal truth and negative truth.

You only know it when you know it. Aloha lives purely by virtue of truth, which is upheld by *pono*, integrity, commitment to harmony and 'making right'. Living in pono is enhancing the joy of the natural sense of integrity, intimacy and simple living and understanding.

Intending...becoming the power of intent within... You then remember the bigger you that you are, who you really are.

It sucks you in until you became indelibly immersed in the sacred sounds of the chants, experiencing extraordinary feelings, mind-boggling things, getting 'chicken skin', seeing, hearing and feeling the stories of drumming and dancing and marching when there is nobody to be seen, and sometimes speaking and chanting in Hawaiian - when we had never learned how...and then, well, we must tell the stories, as stories must be told...

One day we received a phone call from the Hawaiian Chairwoman of the Republican party of Kaua'i. She said,

"I have had a dream. I saw the two of you leading the opening ceremonies, chant and pule (prayers) for the Kaua'i welcoming inauguration of the new Governor. When I told my husband about my dream, he said, "No way, you must be crazy! You know that only a *Kahuna* (priest, wisdom keeper) of traditional rank and stature may perform this ceremony, not *haoles*, blonde foreigners!"

Well, I had the dream again, and I know what that means. It means it will happen. So… will you do it?"

Thus it happened as in her dream; the roomful of hundreds of business leaders stood as if paralyzed in a long stunned silence. This Hawaiian politician/medicine woman had the courage to listen to her dream and to break protocol, in order to honor and value the paradigm of the Unseen world.

Leading our Sacred Sites and Sounds Tour - 2005

I loved nature, and I loved it in its natural wild state. I believed nature loved to be left alone growing wild because that was what I loved the most. One day something happened to change this belief.

I was learning how to prune trees. My teacher, Ken Bernard, was a gardener, - and as I was to discover in time - he was also a geomancer, actually a master of nature's energies. He was explaining and demonstrating how to prune this tree, a tree which was about as tall as me. I watched and listened carefully. Then he walked away, leaving me to work on the next tree on my own.

I stare at it, where do I begin? I circle it, hoping for inspiration to hit me, looking for an opening, a place to start, and a place that calls to me. In spite of his best instruction, I can't figure it out; trying is not working. Knowing I am not getting it I feel frustrated. Is there something wrong with my approach? Where and how should I engage with this tree, - which is after all a living being with a mind of its own. Feeling helpless and disempowered, I start to judge myself, "Elandra, what's the matter with you?"

Suddenly an extraordinary thing happens. All of a sudden I know, I just know exactly what to do, and how to do it! I suddenly know how it would look and feel - how it wants to look and feel. How do I know? I don't know how I know! Perhaps the tree is opening itself to me, inviting me into its energy field.

And then, wow, the tree is communicating with me. Can I say I'm actually hearing it speak to me? Yes! The tree is telepathically sending me messages and understandings.

"Elandra, we know you think nature prefers to be left alone growing wild. We want you to know that's not so. Nature loves to work with humanity. Nature loves the opportunity to co-create together to purify, evolve and beautify life and consciousness in the universe. Because we are actually all a part of each other, we are one with you, made of the same elements, we have a consciousness that becomes one with yours just as you are experiencing now".

As I am receiving this understanding, my hands are easily, readily, surely and masterfully moving from branch to branch, deftly chopping off what wants to be gone. And then comes the most amazing message of all; one that transmits a life changing understanding. The tree continues,

"Elandra, what you are doing right now, chopping off my old dead branches, that's what you do in your healing work. When you oki (chop off, release) the old, then there is room for the new. You have cleared away what no longer serves, making room and space for new branches and new creative growth!

"How do you know exactly what to do? Who guides your hands to work as unerringly as they are doing right now? I am the tree and in becoming one with you, the knowingness is transmitted to you, and you simply know what to do - without knowing how.

"Know that it is exactly the same with you and the body presenting itself on your massage table. This is what you are already doing with your clients. As you oki the body, in the

same way the body has space and energy and room to grow anew. Not only that, but you're clearing old energies from other lifetimes as well, other dimensions, everything that is ready to move, to go, to be released.

"As you do this you're also working through the cells, organs and chakras, and on all levels and layers of the energy field. Then there is room for energy that was lost and given way to return, this is what you call 'soul retrieval'".

Ken and I tell the story of the tree - 2012

This astounding experience gave me a great boost, enabling me to return to my healing work and to stand in an ever more unshakeable confidence in my work. I was learning the art of catalyzing healing, self-healing, in those who came to me. This knowingness was beyond intellect and anything that could be figured out and applied with the mind.

With a sense of great fulfillment inside I went to look for Ken. I just had to show him. I pointed to the tree, standing there radiating balance and harmony, this tree whose universal intelligence had co-created and catalyzed me into being the instrument of its own pruning, and shared so much that was - especially at the time - inexpressible. A big smile on my mouth, pointing at it with supreme delight, I loved feeling invincible in the knowing that there was nothing for him to approve. I knew it was right, it was all pono, just knew, beyond a shadow of a doubt!

I was transformed by this experience. It's not every day that a tree talks to you!

17

My New Work – Lomi Chi Holographic Healing

*Car Accident Brings New Opportunities *Development of Lomi Chi Holographic Healing *Creation of 5th Chakra Holographic Healing *International Training *Miracle Healings*

I didn't talk about to anyone about my experience with the tree, just like I never spoke about those transcendental experiences that continuously guided me towards my destiny as a healer and world teacher. I had almost forgotten about them… those psychics who had shown up out of the blue, as well as Dr. Wendy, Sister Sarita, Louise Hay and Barbara Brennan, (renowned medical intuitive).

In retrospect I see I was being prepared. There was a final major initiation coming my way before becoming an international teacher.

It was a lovely blue sunny day, I had turned out of Aliomanu Road where we lived in Anahola, heading north up the hill, and was driving the gorgeous road north, singing happily on my way to a friend's voice empowerment workshop, little knowing that in just one moment right out of the blue my life would be changed.

The car in front of me is braking, needing to turn off the road, and as I slow down, suddenly - slam bam! I'm rear-ended with tremendous force causing my car to spin several times in the middle of the road and land in a ditch on the other side.

When I come to after blacking out, dazed, body and mind like jelly, I find myself on the other side of the road, the car standing still, very still, facing the wrong way. I open my eyes. I try to open the door, but nothing moves; my body is not obeying my intention and indeed, my whole body is trembling with shock.

Slowly my head, stiffly and painfully, manages to turn, and I observe parked on the other side the car that hit me. There's the driver, sauntering across the street towards me, - what!? He's got a great big grin on his face, why this incongruous big smile? It turns out he's a honeymooning tourist in a rented car. My car is totalled and my neck in severe whiplash.

So now I need a doctor, I don't have a doctor: I'm in my mid-50s, and I've never had a doctor in my life, not in NZ, nor England nor California. My family was never sick, my children were never sick, so why have a doctor…this is a new experience.

The pain in my neck opens me up to my vulnerability. Everything that has ever been "a pain in the neck" all my life is in my face; the unfelt and unexpressed pain of my childhood and inner child helplessness and powerlessness showing up.

I had heard about the fine reputation of Dr. Tom Yarema of Kaua'i Center for Holistic Medicine and Research. Dr. Tom as he was affectionately called was a brilliant medical doctor, emergency room trained, and yet truly holistic, an Ayurveda practitioner, an acupuncturist, a specialist in detoxification, even employing a colon hydro-therapist in his clinic.

I was surprised and deeply touched that this medical doctor knew about the power of prayer, and actually prayed for me, saying "I am always here for you"... It was just what I needed.

As always I dived straight into figuring out what I could learn from this, what are the gifts? I studied whiplash and everything to do with the area of neck and throat. I researched all possible physical problems, mental and emotional, to do with the 5th Chakra, which is the expression of all the other Chakras.

What was still unspoken, repressed in my life?

I had learned so much, from the world's best healer teachers; Barbara Brennan, Pranic Healing, Therapeutic Touch, Lomi Lomi... Chi Nei Tsang from the world's expert, Gilles Marin, Hypnotherapy from Lee Joseph, truth-speaking 'presencing' from Gay Hendricks and much more, way more. Now I found myself in the hands of yet another excellent doctor, chiropractor Dr. Jerry Felcher, who was highly intuitive and encouraging.

It was all coming together. It was time for me to move forward to express even more of my truth, my pain, my fear in life, whatever had been held back. Their work on me gave me my next steps towards the creation and development of the aspect of my work called 5th Chakra Holographic Healing.

Thus the accident and whiplash transformed my life and my work, giving me an inside out deeper understanding: it was my own voice workshop delivered to me. All of this was a fantastic opportunity to learn yet more about healing, and indeed every accident and illness has a gift in it, and is part of the journey from head to heart, the journey of expression of the soul, called the teleology of illness, and understood as such in the ancient ways.

Increasingly, my clients were women with specific needs. They needed to move energy, to express unspoken feelings about the abuse in their backgrounds. After I had incorporated the modality Chi Nei Tsang, (chi through the internal organs) and the tree had spoken to me, my work had taken off, and abdominal Lomi Lomi work became my specialty. Hawaiian women who experienced this work, (there were two in particular who were professional psychics), told me they believed this work was ancient Hawaiian indigenous work which had been lost. One of them, Nahi Guzman, now deceased, named my work "Ho'omana Ke Laka" – the empowerment of Goddess Laka.

I began teaching both healing and women's empowerment workshops. The women's work, called Goddess Embodies later became "WOW, Women of Wisdom", and "WOW! Wildly Organic Women" - but that's a book in itself.

Women of Wisdom - 2004

Watching Dr. Tom and learning from him, first as patient, then as student, I came to believe - along with many of his patients - that he must be the finest doctor in the world. He invited me to become massage therapist at the Kaua'i Center for Holistic Medicine and Research. I loved being part of a team, and I loved inspiring and empowering people. We expanded the Center by acquiring a lecture room for education of the patients and public on all aspects of health. With my yoga and meditation background, as well as the many modalities of healing I had studied, I was in my element.

Unexpectedly yet another opportunity for further learning presented itself. The colon hydro-therapist was leaving; I leapt at the chance to study more about the guts, detoxification and of course my favorite subject, the "second brain", the emotions in the guts, and their functions.

I was surprised at my own enthusiasm and thrilled to be in training eagerly studying every book I could. Who would have thought, a former movie star who could have lived a life of leisure fame, and fortune choosing this instead! Choosing being a healer focusing on detoxing the body - in a way most people consider unmentionable,- dealing with an aspect of the "down there" that nobody talks about!

My father in NZ had been diagnosed with prostate cancer a few years before and was given multitudes of drugs. The drugs caused constipation. High blood pressure followed. More drugs, more constipation. Increasingly constipated, his bowels had become totally impacted and for a year his stool had come out pencil thin. Was there something I could find out that might help him? I didn't want him to die; he was a very healthy 79.

In my healing work I lament that humans have a horror of some aspects of being human. They don't want to know. Mostly they, we, got the message during early toilet training that these parts of ourselves "down there" are dirty, and what comes out is dirty. We learn to be ashamed, and shame is an insidious element of every illness also; shame of being in body, having a body, it goes deep in our western culture. The belief is that spirit and soul is higher; the physical body is low, "down there", dense.

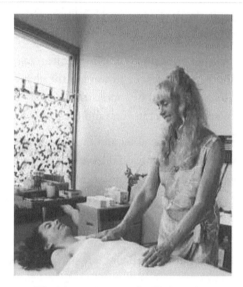

Working at Dr. Tom's Clinic - 2000

Colon therapy is about cleaning the colon, about ridding the body of parasites. The stool is a good indicator of health, and needs to be observed. I would express this to my patients and my enthusiasm must have been contagious; one time a whole family wanted to watch the parasites coming out through the transparent tubes!

A desperate colonic patient flew in from Honolulu. She was seriously constipated, having had no bowel movement for three weeks. She couldn't figure out why. Her abdomen was rock hard, intestines totally impacted. I asked her "What was happening when this began?" "Nothing unusual" she said. Upon further questioning she reluctantly shared that she was angry over being verbally attacked by a neighbor. "I know anger is the worst, really bad, I'm scared of being angry, which means that if I talk back and express my feelings I'll lose my chance at soul redemption – and so might end up in hell."

I said, "We were given anger to use appropriately when we need to. If we hold back and repress our feelings because we believe they're negative, we make ourselves sick."

This lady was a dramatic demonstration of how unconscious belief impacts our physical bodies. She left the clinic a transformed person.

I would lecture to groups about the importance of good elimination for good health, telling my audiences, "If we don't accept all parts of ourselves, then these parts feel unloved and understandably won't function properly. All physical challenges and problems originate in separation, in a lack of self-love and self-acceptance, causing homelessness in the body, especially cancers of the digestive system and reproductive system, especially breast cancer."

I gave mini workshops and talks about the need to cultivate love for ourselves, inside the body as well, love for our insides, intestines, and blood, rather than recoil in fear and horror at the unknown. I would say, "Okay, repeat after me, 'Even though I may not believe it yet, I choose to love all of myself, every part is sacred, I love my elimination, and I love my poop!'" Laughing, we would follow with practicing techniques to generate more loving caring for all the organs and systems in the body.

I tried to tell Dad about colon hydrotherapy, but he didn't want to know. It was too late for him. He was diagnosed with colon cancer and died.

During the many years of living in Hawaii, especially during the six years in Anahola, under the beloved Goddess mountain called Kalalea, I came to live and breathe and be guided by this truth, the Aloha that says "Here we are, breathing the ha, the breath, together, reminding ourselves of our eternal joyful connection through the field, the aka fibers, of our ancestors of light, our Aumakua, our higher selves, our souls.

Kalalea Mountain, Anahola

So Aloha is Hawaii's 'sacred gift' to me. Many come looking for this gift; an attorney turned healer found it and wrote:

"The water of healings is what they called this place where the mountains stood as gentle protectors over a sun soaked inlet of the Pacific. I was here for a reason. I had been introduced to Lomi Lomi massage rooted in the healings of the ancient Hawaiian traditions and was taken by the profound and simple wisdom it reflected. I was drawn to the Hawaiian music that communicated warm breezes from the ocean instead of the choked emission-laden beltway surrounding my home in Washington D.C. Soothed by the simple poetry of the people I wanted to learn more about the touch therapy that quickly enabled me to explore my own soul as effectively as the more ubiquitous disciplines of India and China that have become common in the West.

"I had searched the internet to find my Hawaiian teacher, and dived into the teachings of the islands. Eventually, I took the recommendation of a friend and set off to Kauai. Upon arrival in Hawaii, I had the feeling so common to the breathless ones (that is what we are called by the natives, "haoles") that I was home.

"It did not concern me to learn that the teacher I had scheduled to meet for training needed to cancel. That simply meant she was not my teacher. I spent my days in conversation with a student of Huna and was in awe of the deep respect for nature that permeated this land. It was a few days later that a native Hawaiian recommended that I train with Elandra.

"Elandra did not automatically agree to work with me. In fact, Elandra put me through a few interviews that were as grilling as some of my former attorney interviews. What was it she needed to know? Something I said was the key to an education that would immerse me into the experience of Aloha. Now, a year later, back in Washington, D.C. I know that it is time to share that sacredness with all of the breathless ones who are ready to breathe. I have seen the incredible growth in myself and my clients because of the influence of the ancient teachings and recognize the progress that we could make as a whole (that one whole) by incorporating even a fraction of the simple wisdom of the indigenous people of these islands. I think it is vital and I think we are ready."

After many years of studying with nature and many revered teachers in Hawaii, one day I noticed a shift in my consciousness. I was being interviewed on the radio and suddenly I was no longer afraid of what might come out of my mouth; I didn't care what anybody might hear, say or do in reaction.

I found myself teaching Hawaiian chanting right there while simultaneously thinking "Oh my, who am I - a blonde Scandinavian New Zealander-European Californian ha'ole (without breath, outsider, foreigner) - to do that?"

Even though it was absolutely a 'no-no', I simply had to do what I was doing, say what I was saying, in that moment nothing else mattered. My formerly strangled voice – neck shown in the movies with throat slit and head chopped off - is no longer shackled it is freed! And suddenly I am "home free," finally showing up for myself, speaking my truth.

That was it; I began to be invited to teach internationally.

18

Interviews – Kirsten as the Victim & the Vampire

*The Vampire *Kirsten the Movie Star
*Actress Development and Background
*Hammer Movies *Childhood in Denmark
*Growing up in New Zealand *"What are you becoming?"*

Based on and adapted from *Interview with the First Vampire*

- Oscar Martinez © 2004 Little Shop of Horrors

"The femme fatale is a measure of social change and cultural anxiety. Her incarnations as the witch, the vampire, and the vamp are as much a commentary on history as a representation of the enduring archetypes of sexual women. When she is not at the forefront of cultural expression, she hovers just beneath the surface, awaiting the opportunity to reveal herself again."

--Pam Keesey, *Vamps: An illustrated history of the Femme Fatale*

I picked up the phone one day in 2004, when I was living in Anahola, Kaua'i, and heard, "Are you Kirsten Lindholm, now Elandra Meredith? We would like to request an interview. You may be surprised to know there is a worldwide fan club extremely interested in your movies, especially the Hammer Vampire trilogy".

"Really? Oh my. How amazing. Wow, that was about 30 years ago. I left it all behind and never gave it a thought!"

"I get that. We've been looking for you and just found your website on the internet. Did you know that there are conventions worldwide where your pictures are selling? I heard there was a "bidding war" just for your autograph on a postcard which sold for $60. I am actually a psychologist in New York and together with my mother I've loved your movies since childhood, and I enjoy as a movie buff researching more about how these movies were made, interviewing the actresses and writing about it."

The interview begins with Oscar's introduction (here abbreviated):

"Whenever I read Bram Stoker's Dracula, I always envisioned Kirsten Lindholm as the perfect "Lucy". With her long blond hair and arched dark eyebrows and graceful body movements – lifted from *The Vampire Lovers* in which she plays a vampire sister to Ingrid Pitt's 'Carmilla', the lesbianistic vamp - nobody dons a pair of fangs better.

In the best known movies in which Kirsten appeared, billed as Kirsten Betts and Kirsten Lindholm – *Crescendo*, *The Vampire Lovers*, *Lust for a Vampire*, *Twins of Evil*, her roles were uniquely small in terms of screen time but highly significant to the impact of the films as a whole.

In *Lust For A Vampire* she is the sacrificial virginal victim who sets off the film (the credits pop out of her screaming tonsils) by getting kidnapped and sacrificed in a blood ritual in order to bring life to a vampire – when the vampire emerges from her coffin (Yutte Stensgaard), like her sister in blood, she is a mouth-watering blond more like Kirsten Betts than Ingrid Pitt, as if the source of the blood affected the formulation.

In *The Vampire Lovers* she is the star of the prologue, playing a cat and mouse game with the Shakespearean character of Douglas Wilmer's 'Baron Hartog' as the stunningly lovely vampire who goes on a rampage looking for her shroud. The prologue sequence in fact so telegraphed the rest of the plot (stoic vampire hunter chasing after a vampire whose weapon included mesmerizing the viewer with her beauty, and, closing it off with her gruesome and unexpected decapitation) to the point where the critics of the times mentioned that the rest of the film, after the opening credits, never quite achieved the impact of the prologue....

But her impact and influence appear to have set the tone for the trilogy. She became, as it were, the representative idea and imagery of the Karnstein family of vampires. As a prototype, the 'First Vampire' in the Carmilla Karnstein trilogy became the model from which the other vampire women in the trilogy would be derived.

To track a vampire: Like the sister of Carmilla Karnstein, the real Kirsten disappeared, jointed a cult and dressed in white and like Carmilla she reappeared later, under another name, still just as beautiful, but this time giving life as a health healer and teacher of yoga in a Polynesian island in Hawaii.

When you learn more about Kirsten – that she was born in the land of fairy tale spinner Hans Christian Andersen – you will still be mesmerized. Up to be a James Bond girl – having been spotted in the Hammer Horrors by Harry Saltzman and Albert ("Cubby") Broccoli – she upped instead to disappear on a soul searching expedition that changed her life forever.

Oscar: Your website is amazing. You are a healer and a teacher. And you were born in the land of fairy tales, Denmark, country of the famous Hans Christian Andersen. Since this interview is primarily on the films you made for Hammer Productions in the early 1970's, I find it fascinating that you and your life and everything that that means appears to encompass a rich production of fantasy (in a most realistic sense) from present and lengthy success as a healer and teacher, to the background as an actress.

Kirsten: It never occurred to me to consider my life as "a rich production of fantasy!" I was born in the land of fairy tales, indeed in the very same town as Hans Christian Andersen and lived close by his house in my first six years of life before my family immigrated to New Zealand.

Oscar: Hans Christian Andersen is indeed an icon of Denmark. Without diverting into mawkishness, I must say that in terms of physical attributes you present an exceedingly attractive woman and, in some regards, some of your life has an enchantment and aura akin to one of Hans Christian Andersen's fairy tales.

Kirsten: It's interesting to consider how much Denmark as my birthplace, my love for it, and these stories were so influential in my life. Enchantment.... Yes, I probably took on this fairy tale conviction that anything is possible! Perhaps that is also part of the reason my healing work and teaching is so successful now, although I was not aware of having a fantasy of being a healer as such. In fact, a lot of the time my world didn't feel that magical at all, in spite of the "physical attributes!" No wonder I have had these experiences of amazing miracle healings!

One thing is for sure, I had an extraordinary imagination, perhaps nurtured by these tales. And this made up for, and was even the result of the lack of physical toys and books in early 1950s New Zealand. There was so much magic in my imagination, and tremendous longing and curiosity. I have very clear memories of growing up in Denmark. We had left to be pioneers in a new world, but we clung to Denmark emotionally, it was our homeland, and all the Danes in NZ referred to it as hjem - home.

Oscar: It must have been quite a journey in those days to move to New Zealand, a country where you knew nobody and spoke no English. Later you became an award-winning academic scholar and a prize-winning ballroom dancer, even winning the World Championships in Formation Team Ballroom Dancing in Australia. What was all of that like for you?

Kirsten: It was an amazing transition to leave one country for another. Born during the war in the early grim times of occupied Denmark, I remember the fear, shooting in the streets, banging on our door, rations, nothing much to eat, no toys. I've always had this awe and admiration for my father (an unschooled farmer's son) for the courage it took to, first of all, to even dare to dream of a better life, and then to move heaven and earth to make it happen. That meant working a full day job as well as a night watchman job for years to get the whole family on an ocean liner heading for the far reaches of the planet. We left for the unknown having no idea if we would ever see our large loving families again.

Out of necessity I read comics and in short order was top of the class in all subjects, a position I held throughout my school career. No toys, no TV, no computer games, no phone, no car, nothing to do but study! Also there were very few books available, and out of sheer boredom as well as my lifetime craving for knowledge, I read a twelve volume encyclopedia on astronomy at age nine. At high school I was Vice Captain of the Hockey Team and loved and excelled in all sports including dancing, and received the highest marks ever given in NZ for all levels of ballroom dancing. We won the World Championship Formation Team Competition in Australia.

Oscar: You also majored in languages?

Kirsten: I spent years learning English, German, French and then a year of Swedish (I was raised speaking Danish) language and literature. In fact I took the academic life so seriously that I became deeply disillusioned and depressed at university by what seemed the shallowness of being there just to pass exams!

And I had this fantasy of being the serious scholar by day and a different creature by night, wildly dancing the night away! Whether at a nightclub or ballroom, I relished stopping everybody in their tracks to watch me spinning and flying around the dance floor. (Later, when living in the heart of London in Mayfair my nights were spent in the same way, dancing till dawn in the fashionable 'in' places!)

I recently returned from a teaching trip to Germany (I am being invited to teach all around the world), and found all those years pouring over books weren't wasted after all! It was so much fun being able to understand and reconnect with that long forgotten intellectual scholar in me!

Oscar: Was it then in New Zealand that you started in modeling and print and television advertising commercials? Tell me about that period of your life.

Kirsten: I was modeling for TV commercials, hair shampoo and stuff. My very first modeling job was for girdles; they were enormous, as I had such a slim torso and waist. I just drowned in them and they had to pad them out! A ridiculous deception, as advertising is!

I took acting and dance classes, and began acting, for example, in a Revue as the Goldfinger girl, and in German plays such as lead in Berthold Brecht *Mann ist Mann*. I loved it and danced spontaneously in it. They called me 'Legs Andreassen' because the publicity photos showed my long slim legs; they were blown up into huge posters and they couldn't keep those posters up, they were always disappearing off the walls.

Within the walls of academia I met a fellow actor, a Professor of Latin and Greek, a nice Englishman who impressed me with his Greek dancing. I just knew, strangely, I was going to marry him. My parents put on a grand wedding, and I left NZ never to return to live, at least so far.

Oscar: It was around 1966, the height of the 'Swinging London' scene that you arrived in England. Speak about that whole period and its atmosphere. What were you after, what were you searching for, and what did you experience?

Kirsten: I'll never forget my first day in London. I was utterly blown away with the sense of possibility. The air vibrating with the excitement of big city life, culture, the arts, ballet, architecture, everything I was longing for must be here! And it was. This was the wild 'Swinging London' of the 60s and early 70s, those amazing years of 'flower power' and freedom which many look back upon with nostalgia.

There's a video and book called *Flashing on the 60s* which brings back those heady times, including the yoga I got into. I was looking for my European roots; I was crazy for both learning and adventure. Every night I was at the theatre, watching Margot Fonteyn and Nureyev, or at glitzy events meeting the Royal family or stars of stage and screen. There I was, a conservative innocent from the far reaches of the world, just showing up, and meeting my agent while crossing Park Lane one day!"

Oscar: You were born Kirsten Lindholm Andreassen. Later your name was Kirsten Betts. Now it is Elandra Meredith or Elandra Kirsten Meredith. Your website notes that the name Betts came from your marriage to John Betts, an English professor of Latin and Greek. Betts was the name you used in 1970 when you starred in *The Vampire Lovers*. In *Lust for a Vampire* (also 1970) and *Twins of Evil* (1971) your on screen last name is Lindholm. Tell me about the history of your names?

Kirsten: When I married in NZ I became Kirsten Betts. Later, as the marriage was ending, I chose to again use my original name, and for simplicity's sake I chose to leave off Andreassen. Then I got my third name… you didn't mention! How I came by this name, Vikram Kaur, is also the story of how I came to disappear from London and the entertainment field, suddenly and unexpectedly, leaving behind the career my agents and I had worked for over the years. It started with a yoga class. I was open to and looking for something…I walked into a whole new world that day. The atmosphere of eager voluntary discipline, devotion and peace was mind blowing. I didn't know what to think, but I knew what my parents and everyone I knew would think about me being there. Weird!

Well, this was not yoga as generally understood in these days of fashionable popularity. Students were not there for stress release and stretching or to be seen in the most fashionable gear. This was life-changing Kundalini Yoga.

Within a year, I was married again, had a new name, (the same as my new husband's, only he was Vikram Singh (lion of invincibility) and I Vikram Kaur(princess of pure invincibility of action) was a trained yoga teacher in California, in white clothes, married, pregnant, living in an Ashram Yoga Center community with some 30 yogi devotees.

I had arrived in April 1972 in LA where I was going for a quick trip with my yoga teacher, to see his teacher. I expected to return to London shortly. It all happened so fast. I never even called my acting agent, nor my modeling agent, nor anybody else

I have since learned that one's name carries a vibration, a frequency. I didn't intend to change it again, what a hassle to do legally! Never again! But there I was with my fourth name, Elandra Kirsten Meredith, which means to me "the power of love and wisdom," and "guardian of the seas of consciousness." Neither parents, customs, laws nor Guru – this time I named myself! Actually it just popped in while I was eating breakfast one day, and I knew this was it; this was my real name.

Oscar: Now I want to ask you a series of questions, some of which may sound almost interrogative, because they have to do with a deep concentration on the Hammer Productions that you did. Judging from the wonderful work that you have been doing for the last 30 years in healing and teaching, they may sound almost frivolous. But I guarantee you they are not. You may or may not know this but if you throw the name Kirsten Betts into the Internet and if you go to the index of scholarly books on the history of the horror film, the bit that you did in the prologue of *The Vampire Lovers* is probably one of the most talked about and most quoted about scenes. So I will start by asking you, first and foremost, do you feel that your appearances in the Hammer Productions were in fact frivolous, when you remember them now in retrospect?

Kirsten: Let's see…the word "frivolous" means to me something like unconsidered, non-serious, perhaps inconsequential…In those days it seemed like life was just happening to me, and I was running to receive what it brought to me, not really knowing what I was doing, what I wanted to grow up to be!

And in a way it's still that way, always changing, but with much more awareness! But in retrospect…when I was 17 or so I remember a visitor came to my house, looked at me with this prophetic awe, and said "You have both brains and beauty; you have the whole world at your feet!"

I knew it was true, and it overwhelmed me. It felt like a burden trying to satisfy so many parts of me. I wished for some direction, clarity, fewer confusing choices. Yet simultaneously, my life always seemed so "on purpose," as if guided somehow in my continuing journey of self-realization.

Much later when I opened to the more empowered part of me (that healed my broken ankle overnight - that's a story!) and realized I had the power to heal others in miraculous ways, I started to have some past life recall, remembering that I had once been called a witch and burned at the stake for such powers.

I remembered my part in *Twins of Evil* being burnt at the stake. I shivered; it was for real! I wondered at the miraculous synchronicity of life that had me acting out my own past life time realities on the screen.

And in my development as a powerful healer these past 16 years I have had to go through the fears around death and dying in horrible ways (because on this lonely path of self-training you have to face all your fears) in those selfsame ways yet again. Well, I had no idea at the time of the significance of my appearances in these movies, and here it is showing up years later, talking to you, so no, not frivolous!

Oscar: Hollywood legends are often described as being "loved" by the camera. When you were on camera, all eyes were on you. Roy Ward Baker, the director of *The Vampire Lovers* says in the 2003 USA DVD release of the film that he felt that since you were cast as what would be called the "First Vampire," that is, the first vampire that would be seen on the screen in that movie, that he needed someone who would be (1) visually striking and (2) someone who could move well. Comment on this, that is, your photogenic quality (which is still striking in the photos on your website on the healing) and your ease with movement, which I would imagine, has to do with your background as a dancer. And were those traits significantly related in your casting?

Kirsten: Before I ever took any dance classes I was just naturally very limber and athletic. I loved all forms of movement and felt very at home in my body. I felt that I could have been a gymnast or ballet dancer. People speak of my charisma, and magnetism, or power of presence...I am really only now trying to understand and accept that! Well, a part of me is...so that is perhaps what Roy Ward Baker recognized, along with the "ease of movement," and "photogenic quality." Often when I would appear for an interview I would be greeted with the comment, "Wow, you are even more beautiful in real life!" What real beauty really is, and does, is an ongoing mystery, because for me –at the time – beauty didn't have to do with acting!

To me real acting was what was happening when I was in the Masked Theatre Company doing Shakespeare in small theatres in and around London, behind a mask, rather than appearing on stage or screen for my looks! Occasionally in my workshops an energy blasts through that astounds people. In Hawaii we call it *mana*, a kind of authentic mysterious power.

Oscar: Tell me about Antion and your life now. How does he react to this interest in the horror films that you did once upon a time?

Kirsten: I asked him, my husband of 32 years, what do you think about the current fascination for these movies? He said, "I see in these movies a certain combination of beauty, innocence, sensuality that actually was reflective of the times of the seventies. We are presented with women as innocent victims along with the charged dangerous "femme fatale." The vampire femme fatale is a woman who is a source of mystery and fascination for men. And for women she's a source of fascination as a symbol of power and freedom, one who has set herself free of conventional stereotypes of good nice girl virtue, no longer being part of society's mores of what she is supposed to be, so that may be part of the fascination...sounds like you Elandra!"

So it's amazing because it all fits into the ongoing discussion of our lives ...In the women's liberation "burn your bra" times of the 70s, I had decided never to get married and have children; instead I wanted what it seemed my mother didn't have, autonomy, independence, respect, freedom. What I did have, an innocent beauty, I didn't want to wield as power. I could walk into a room and have every man not only want me but be willing to do anything to get me, including leave his wife. I didn't like this kind of power! And I didn't want to use it, knowing I would end up despising everything that came to me this way.

I did want to develop true empowerment, become femme fatale in the sense of being a "woman unto myself beyond definition and beyond control, dedicated to a higher purpose," to use Pam Keesey's words from Vamp, *An Illustrated History of the Femme Fatale*.

What happened was Antion was like the Pied Piper for me; he was my yoga teacher in 1969. I fell in love with his singing. I had a vision of his music helping change the world, and 32 years of marriage later, I continue to be wild about him! He sings about the Goddess and so people say I am his Goddess. Our picture is on the *One in The Goddess* CD cover on the beach where we live. I rather liked it that our daughter's friend asked "Is that your father's girlfriend?"

In those days I showed up in his yoga classes in the fashions of the time, hot pants, miniskirts, transparent blouses, and long eyelashes. He was the first man that I knew who deliberately ignored me, which in itself sparked my interest!

These days he presents his unique blend of Hawaiian and Indian devotional songs, and sometimes I dance Hula with his music. We lead Sacred Sites and Sounds Journeys into the magic and mystery of ancient

Hawaii, he teaches Voice Empowerment and Sacred Voice Healing Seminars, and we present workshops together.

Oscar: How do you feel about this type of interviewing and fan focus on your Hammer films?

Kirsten: I'm surprised at how I'm enjoying it. I like you and Dick and Nancy Klemensen and *Little Shoppe of Horrors* magazine.

Making these movies was fun; there was an unusual sense of goodwill, a sort of family feeling, and it is enjoyable to remember this. This is reflected in the appeal of this magazine, called horror but not evil horror, the good wins out, all somehow with a degree of good humor and heart. I am also enjoying it from the perspective of it being part of the making of the person I am becoming!

Oscar: As we come to an end of this first section of the interview, I want to know, what are you becoming, Elandra? What is your next adventure?

Kirsten: I've enjoyed this, Oscar; it helps me to come to terms with all parts of myself, - an ongoing work of the inner Goddess! I never know where it will lead me, and that's the adventure and the joy of the journey! I look forward to more.

On the beach at Kihei, Maui, photo by Virginia St.Claire

19

Reflections: Being Here Now

*What is Authentic *The Nature of Beauty*
*Identity *Where Are We Going as a World?*
*Voices of Sacred Earth *Wonder and Awe*
WOW!

"The planet does not need more successful people. The planet desperately needs more peacemakers, healers, restorers, storytellers and lovers of all kinds."

--Dalai Lama

"The longing to increase individual possessions is a serious deterrent to our real expansion, spiritually and personally."

--Makua, Hank Wesselman, *Bowl of Light*

"Presencing is the act of resting your attention on something real that you're experiencing right now."

--Gay and Kathlyn Hendricks, *Spirit-Centered Relationships*

"When mankind accepts the Goddess there'll be Love, Light and Peace"

--Antion

Elandra's Holo-Perception

If people were living more simply and more in touch with the earth then in one or two generations we would have an entirely different world. Can you imagine how programmed we are to believe that happiness is in having more and more 'economic growth' called 'civilization'? Current research tells us humanity has lost its way, 'science' and 'progress' has brought nothing sustainable and maintainable for our health and happiness and that of the earth. In the USA what is spent on war in one single day is more than enough to feed and take care of the whole of the world's population.

As Krishnamurti said, "It is no measure of good health to be well adjusted to a profoundly sick society". People struggle to keep up with this contrived manipulated-by-others reality, wondering why they can't find financial security, a permanent partner, or physical health, fitness, slimness, or peace of mind and happiness. It's a false existence of false and artificial values that's called economic growth, and designed to bamboozle us into a lifetime of debt and divorce, which neither brings nor supports balance, love and happiness, and leaves people sick and miserable at the end of their life wondering what it was all about on their deathbed, if indeed they have any consciousness left at all in their Alzheimer's riddled brains.

The reason it is so hard to imagine is that we are a deliberately monetized and commoditized money-driven culture from beginning to end.

This chapter is based on and adapted from an interview for Beatrice Maddach's short film, *"Change in Progress".*

Growing Up

As I was growing up there was always a part of me thinking, "I've got to remember what remembering is like." You know the Hansel and Gretel story where they realize they don't know where they are going in the forest and had better be able to find the way back, and so get the idea to make a track by dropping crumbs along the way that they can follow later, before the crumbs disappear eaten by birds. It's like I was trying to do that, find a way to return to that place I came from, as if my journey here to this earth was also a journey home.

Deliberately Remembering what it's like Being a Child

As soon as I could write at age six I was writing lists and goals for myself, all the things I wanted to do. At age 11 I had a journal of my feelings and I wrote that it's very important to remember what it was like being born and being a child, and I was writing this because I wanted to make sure that I wouldn't forget that I was here for a reason and I was trying to find out what it was, always looking for something.

My Beloved Parents

My parents worked so hard, first to make it through the war, get to NZ, and then in a new country to make it and to feed and launch three kids; they were incredible parents and did so much for us and my love and admiration for them knows no bounds.

Later I learned my father was an accomplished horseman, my mother an artist, but I didn't see that growing up, I saw them working full time and sacrificing for us. After a while we connected with other Danes, and the Danish community meant a lot, they became family. But still, just working so much, and maybe when you do that you have to just keep going, what it takes, to have a nice big house, and the expectations...

But it took all their energy. It was a powerful European work ethic which contrasted with the laid back way of the islanders. In those days they didn't have much opportunity for vacations and relaxing, no hanging out at a beach with hula girls and bananas you could reach out for. I guess it's all about finding a balance.

Looking for Wisdom and Belonging

I went through University thinking: I'm going to find some wisdom here. I'm going to find the something that I'm looking for. I was reading Goethe, Nietzsche and Schopenhauer and studying all the great masters of literature, along with History and Theory of Fine Arts and finding out that that the great writers and artists wanted to take off, get out of this world, wanted to die. They wanted to commit suicide and I thought, that's a good idea, because I feel like I too don't belong here. So that was where my consciousness was at, having a lot of empathy for their suffering, and at the same time seemingly having a life full of accomplishment, success and opportunity as a top student. So if in the intellectual world wisdom was not to be found, then where?

Get a Husband with Money

What I saw and learned as a girl in our society was - get a husband, one who makes money. Women can't take care of themselves; they're bad drivers, and thus incompetent; not much good at anything other than taking care of the home.

Materialism the Hallmark of our Culture

I noticed everything becoming more and more covered over with concrete, roads, houses, more and more suburbia, the pristine beaches becoming surrounded with more and more miles of buildings. All considered desirable, growth was the goal, no matter what. Even back then in those days, at age 16, 17, 18, I was becoming horrified by the materialism, the focus on more, bigger and better; it was survival of course, but also the hallmark of our culture.

Decision to be Different

What's life about? I'm never going to live like this. I'm never going to live in a regular house, raising kids in suburbia. For what? No way! But in those days if you didn't get married, it was like, oh, you're on the shelf, very embarrassing, a failure, bringing shame to the family and failing them in their expectations. Getting married was the thing to do, you had to.

My First True Love – Yogananda

I was always looking for something, as if home were not here, a part of me just wanted to find my way back home. And I certainly wasn't finding it in my parents or anywhere around me, not even at University until I found a book, Yogananda's book, Autobiography of a Yogi. I tore out the picture of him and hung it in a secret place inside my closet. Then I started having visions of India.

Always Looking

When I landed in London I got a great burst of energy, wow! I loved it! Without even looking I started working right away as an actress, small roles but always with famous actors. The very first was Gregory Peck and it went on from there. But still, I was always looking, everywhere looking, visiting all the art galleries and architecture of Europe looking...for something.

Who is the Real Me?

I felt, hey, I'm so alone here, I want the real me to be seen! The closest that I could get to that was to be intellectual, and so I was always studying, learning; everything fascinated me. I saw myself in a dichotomy: on the one hand, as an intellectual by day, and on the other, as the wild dancing one at night!

There was nobody that I could relate to who could really understand that. We all want to be seen, don't we? Acknowledged and appreciated for who we really are - whatever that is. Because we don't know yet at that age and when do we know?

Touching the Unknown - Masked Theatre Company

But the most exciting thing wasn't working with the famous; I wasn't that impressed. It was rather performing Shakespeare in a Masked Theatre Company that I joined. Because under those masks it was like my - whoever I thought I was - my identity - was hidden and so I could be ...whatever, something other than what I thought I was. And in rehearsal our director who was Greek encouraged this, so these voices would come out of me and everyone else too. We'd be doing spontaneous stuff and actually in a way it was channeling! That was the closest I got to something...

I was still looking I didn't know for what... My mother was a bit of an atheist, anything spiritual was anathema to her, and I too was horrified by anything to do with proselytizing religions.

Power of Beauty and "Sex Symbol"

As a blonde Scandinavian sex symbol I got an instant "in," became very successful, even when there were 40,000 actors out of work at the time. But I was uncomfortable with having more and more men falling all over themselves for me. I always had to deal with that and what that meant. And the fascinating thing was I didn't understand this thing called beauty. I never considered myself beautiful. Just didn't know what it was. I admired and pursued intellect as the highest consciousness. Brains not beauty because "you couldn't have both" was the prevalent belief.

So I felt a bit (especially in interviews for castings or modeling jobs) like meat market-looked-over - the whole thing to do with looks. I hated the vibe, the competition aspect, the cut-throat feel, and more and more I wanted to be seen not for my looks but for me, the real authentic me, even though I didn't know what that was.

I've been made aware since that there is something very powerful about beauty, a woman's beauty especially and the effect of beauty on men. It's transcendent, magical, not just attraction, nor just sexual attraction. It's not just a lower chakra lust thing.

It's deeper, perhaps a longing for the respect, valuing and honoring of true feminine energy that is so missing on the planet. Beauty speaks to the soul and so it's a very high thing. That pornography is the greatest income maker in the whole world, and human trafficking next to it, shows how far our world has come from respect and sacredness.

I have more understanding and more compassion in a sense too now. I think continually shifting along with my understanding. I couldn't really…I mean… I was beautiful. I didn't know it then and didn't believe it, but I was. Every single part and inch of me was but I couldn't relate to it. And so in a way I turned my back on understanding that whole thing.

Dancing in the surf, Maui - 2010

Yoga and Seeking the Authentic Self

My first experience of something more authentic was what I experienced at the yoga centre. Not that I was being 'seen' in that sense. I was just a student arriving at Vikram Singh's yoga class but…there was a sense of something higher there than me… the music he would play afterwards, the Americans there, the sharing, and I'd feel that this is somehow the answer.

Those were exciting times in the wild 60s, but there was so much I didn't know being just an innocent "babe in the woods" fresh from NZ. And I had no way of relating to all this, always putting on a show, acting confident but adrift inside, alone in London. Having men always hitting on me, I suppose to the ego it was okay, but I was deeply uncomfortable and bewildered and at a loss to know how to deal with it. I mean I was such a softhearted person. I couldn't say no very easily, and I couldn't lie.

Schools Need to Teach Real Life Relationship

Wouldn't it be great if we learned in school more about male-female energies and relationships, how to relate! What ego is, how to communicate, meeting needs, finding fulfillment, all of that? I was totally in the dark about all this, just as was my mother, and so were those I knew and called my friends.

Lonely with No Real Friends

Sadly there actually were none of those; I was not really close to anyone, and later realized women were jealous of me, and I couldn't understand that, because jealousy, what was that?

Valuing Inner Beauty

So that aspect of it, what was going on was puzzling to me, and dissatisfying. Perhaps that partly explains how I could find myself within a short time looking for inner beauty, and ending up covered head to toe in white clothes. One benefit was that it helped me remove the focus on outer appearance, and helped me focus my energy inside instead. At high school we wore uniforms, and I liked that I didn't have to pay attention to what I would wear that day; the decision was made already, it simplified life, and so I could focus more on my studies.

In the same way being in a group where the prescribed dress is a loose shapeless garb meant that I didn't have men after me all the time, which helped me be inside, exploring what was there, rather than attracting people with my appearance. The inside was important, my relationship to my inner being and my energy field, along with the strength and power in the sense of belonging.

Spiritual Practice

It's like depositing into a bank account – the energy of doing it – the more you do the more you have in there to draw upon. I felt all this power inside me building up, like, there's nothing I can't do.

It's called mana. You know when you hear stories of women picking up cars off their children - that kind of energy; it's the "double" or "second self" that merges with the body in a crisis situation. I didn't know about that then.

And so the outside reflected that with the white clothes but it's quite extreme to do that as my mother would sorrowfully - or angrily - point out. There was a lot of good in it, as a focus that supported not living from the lower chakras, but as we were saying spiritual practice by itself didn't do the emotional healing.

How Could You Leave What is Everybody's Dream - Celebrity?

I meet people who are trying so hard to make it in movies or entertainment industry. They literally think I am crazy when they hear I walked away from it all. Walked away from what they are desperate for! They look at me as if to say what a fool! You must be making it up. It doesn't compute, they think I'm lying. They would give anything to be a successful movie star, or even a make-up artist, a screen writer or playwright. In my whole life, so much in my life, people don't believe who I am. Or what I do.

Giving Away My Power

During my years in the organization in many ways I was giving away my power to another set of beliefs. Even though it was a high one, it was still another authoritarian belief system.

Yet perhaps that's what I had to do to end up healing and balancing myself, - which I continue to work on. (Working on with all of that knowledge that is coming together to publish in books).

In line with what I was told, I wore white, but these days I rarely wear white, rather I love wearing very bright colors especially violet, purple, and turquoise. I feel that they feed me and my aura, while white feels rather anemic making. We have to decide for ourselves.

What is the Ideal Spiritual Teacher

I like what Einstein said, "I have reached an age when, if someone tells me to wear socks, I don't have to." Until you get there, ideally the teacher that you would have is one who says, "This is the most important as a discipline but ultimately what it's about is finding your own true self in relationship to it." We've become quite aware of how gurus have come over from India and just suck the energy and money out of their students and disciples who end up bowing to them and giving away all their power.

Addiction

And we have seen those perhaps originally good teachers become power hungry themselves. It's addiction, more and more, more and more cult consciousness. I learned a great lesson from that, an extremely painful lesson - as the best ones are!

Authoritarianism

There's no doubt it's a long journey to get to the heart from the head, because at the beginning we are students, and so we obey the orders from above to find true discipline. Consciousness of abuse and authoritarianism has come a long way. The need to actually feel feelings instead of suppressing them is vitally important. That's where I've come to now.

Welcoming Feelings

And that's what I'm practicing and teaching now - welcoming those feelings instead of immediately wanting to get rid of them, whether that's by running to the fridge or smoking or drugs or whatever. Even immediately wanting to get rid of them by turning yourself positive. That isn't the best way of handling them either.

Perceptions and Unconscious Belief

By affirming saying, "I'm healthy, I feel fantastic, I'm great, I have lots of money" - whatever the good affirmations are, the 95% (because we're 95% unconscious as Bruce Lipton, *Biology of Belief*, tells us) will say, "No, you're lying!" And so it'll probably make you sicker. But I think that's come to be quite well understood now, that such affirmations need to include our sub-personalities' subconscious beliefs. The call is to fearlessly face the negative feelings repressed and hidden within, rather than pretend they don't exist.

Cultural PTSD

I believe USA or western culture is in permanent cultural post-traumatic stress syndrome. It needs healing big time. We all have traumas; it's inevitable. Society, the world we live in, even if it's not that personal and individual, trauma is part of society. It's in the airwaves. It's the collective consciousness and collective unconscious. You can't avoid it. We think that the more we think we're healed the better off we are, and that's true of course, but most of all, the more we recognize how much there still is to go, the more the energy can flow! What you feel you can heal. What you resist persists. Of course that idea can be misunderstood; there are times when full on resistance is necessary being self-defense in the face of abuse.

The Importance of Play in Developing Imagination and Agelessness

One day I was playing with my little nephew, a 7-year-old little boy and he told his mother, "I love my auntie because she plays like a kid." I thought, hey, best compliment ever! And well maybe that's why he feels that way, because back then I just resolved that I wasn't going to forget what it's like to be a kid… and to play, and to use imagination, and so I can relate on his level. Einstein said something incredibly powerful when he said that "Imagination is more important than knowledge", but we know our society has lost it in the pushing to make unbalanced left -brain -exam -passing robots out of all of us.

The Secrets to Ageless Living

The result is that it's in the subconscious response to the healing, that the body becomes healthier and then totally healthy. Not having reached 100 years old yet I don't know from experience, but I do know from experience that at my age now in my 60s I feel like a 20-30-year-old. And I can run just as fast as this 7-year-old kid and climb trees and roll down hills. We were doing it yesterday. That's what I feel is the secret to ageless living. I know that I have to be that youthful and playful. So what does that mean further on? That's what I'm really excited about, that's why I'm full time researching this topic.

Death and Dying in Our Culture – Needs a Makeover!

Okay, I feel strongly about this, the process of both birth and death needs a great upgrade of awareness in our culture. Neither birth nor dying belong in a hospital for the sick. I don't intend to lie around in a hospital bed when it's my turn to go. A lot of us "cultural creatives" feel that way so we will see. I mean if I had a car accident - fine, I'd be very grateful to be taken to hospital, that's really what it's for, a patching up place, not a healing place.

We're baby boomers seeing our parents nearing the end of their time and passing over, and learning that – hey, we're not going to do it their way, miserable on our backs in a hospital bed being told how great palliative care is! No way I say. I saw what goes on - first-hand, watching Mum in hospital. Terrible, it's not at all what they say! Go research this yourself, go to the hospitals, retirement villages and hospices before you have to! And in order to choose something different! And as for pain killers, none were working for Mum, not the strongest that were permitted by law!

The thing is that a lot of terminally suffering people desperately want to die – by choice and in dignity and at home, but often are not permitted by law. This is saddest thing, and a huge topic.

The fact is that as things are, our bodies belong to the state and you don't have much say, and you have to fight for your say. Everybody needs to write a "final directive" or "living will" or Five Wishes, and have it on file in the event of being unconscious. Do you want to be kept alive on feeding tubes in a coma for years? No matter our age or health, we could be in an accident unable to state our wishes. Do it now I always say.

Birth and death need to be faced, honored as sacred, not drugged away, whimpered away, and turned from in fear. I don't fear death because I don't believe there is death of consciousness. My challenge would be the fear of being unconscious in a living death, say in a coma, in an unconscious world.

Inner Self-Healing

Everything else, every other form of disease – we've got a lot of shame and toxins and a lot to deal with but we can work with it by learning how to heal on the inner with the trauma, by dealing with the subconscious stuff, the inner unconscious perceptions turned beliefs that actually run our lives. This takes ongoing work and focus. Most importantly, it takes asking for help. Have you noticed how hard it is to ask for help? So much shame and pride in there!

The Best Health Insurance

We don't have to manifest a physical disease. Everything can be self – healed. The best health insurance and the only one I have ever had is good nutrition, exercise, emotional healing, meditation, speaking the truth and such. When you meditate you are in touch with self, when you don't others control you and your thoughts and beliefs. When you pay for health insurance then maybe you'd better get sick to get your money's worth?! The system is based in fear. Crazy. Learn instead, study. Study the body and learn the truth about your body.

Mind Control and "Normalcy Bias"

The change that's coming is so huge that people cannot accept it, because we've been brought up, brainwashed, conditioned and mind controlled to certain – unconscious - perceptions and beliefs. The beliefs are that this kind of thing, natural healthy living and miracle healing, is impossible. And this conviction causes utmost pathology; it causes the worst of the worst to be happening in our world. Causes addiction to war, power, right? It's fear and that's just part of it.

Here on the Planet for What?

I don't know the answer for others, only for myself. We have come here for a purpose. There is no such thing as idly playing harps in heaven, all life is about evolution. What did we come here for? We must have come here to explore all this, make choices, and develop character. We must have come here to be part of seeing or creating the worst of the worst, so that we could find the best of the best. It must be what the world is about.

Well, we're doing it to learn. We chose it to learn, and to serve and evolve and remember all of who we are. We wouldn't be here right now if it weren't for that. And we are having fun, aren't we? Right now we're having fun. I love talking about this stuff!

And seeing it in front of me - not everyone has that experience - but right in front of my own eyes I get to see broken bones healed instantly? Out of that experience of conviction I have something to share, and I get to share it a lot. My whole work developed around that, and I've touched thousands of people with this understanding.

And you read about people having NDEs, near death experiences, where they leave the body and they come back full of joyful knowledge and understanding of the other side and why we're all doing this. And so all we can do is just keep coming back to that touchstone. It's hugely inspirational to read the stories, and to use them to support us in times of trouble.

Reality of Two Worlds

So these are the two realities that I was talking about… one is a truth consciousness reality, the Unseen, and the other is what they call "the real world" the Seen. The Unseen is really the real world. It's a total reality to me and that reality can be transmitted. We all live in a field of energy, a morphogenetic field. And so a transmission is occurring all the time when people are open. For someone like me, who's having an experience like that when I'm in the presence of my client, student or a group of people, then my energy is a transmission, even if it's not in a conscious, deliberate way, even if it's anonymous. Even if nobody knows, it still is. It's still happening.

Beginning with Willingness, Openness and Readiness

Then sometimes it happens with my clients and students also when the willingness, openness and readiness is there. I lead them into a place where they are no longer focused in their heads. All that conditioning I was talking about is released with a little bit of hypnotherapy we might call it, with techniques that allow the head, the brain, the mind, to relax out of its feeling that it's the only thing, it's the biggest thing, it's the most valued thing in society… so then when that part relaxes a little bit then the field, the other parts, the cells, all are a little more open and they can receive that reality.

It's pretty amazing, isn't it? Every story like this and there are plenty of them in the world! - every story brings us closer to valuing something other than the rational mind, and that is the change. And as we learn to value intuition and feelings and body and value body as barometer of feelings, or as a message maker, as we learn to value something other than brain/head as priority, that's it!

The Sacred Gift

This is what Einstein meant when he spoke of "the sacred gift". He was obviously a visionary mystic. He knew all of this way back then. And in spite of that we've gone through a world that's conditioned to not believe anything other than what we are told by authorities. So anyway, every story, every moment where we can share this kind of thing makes a difference. It does make a difference, that's what I keep getting - and saying.

Disgusted at this World

There are moments where I feel really, they're less and less, but I get very disgusted and horrified at humanity. And then all I hear from within are messages saying, "Just embrace, be open to love, love, love, ever more." How can we love stuff like that? How can we love the worst of the worst? And yet that's the answer.

Love is the Key

I do know that love is the key, to face and embrace love in the face of all, and to obey love. Mathew Fox talks about this: "We live in the midst of a suicidal economy, motivated by love of money. We have reached a dead end. What we need to turn it around are hearts in love with life. How do we do it? We first must move from domination to partnership, and we begin by educating our young in awe and wonder, not how to take tests. Awe leads to reverence, which leads to gratitude, which will reinvent our species. This is the task of our generation: to regain awe".

The Goddess

To me the Goddess is the embodiment of Aloha. To me this is not an idea. It's reality! This is 'the real world'. How else does miracle instant healing happen? Of course it may take time to feel it as reality, to know it in every fiber of your bones, cells and being. Or - it could happen in an instant! It's a personal decision.

It may come through your choice to accept the call, the kahea, to embark upon the traditional "hero's journey", which will lead you to ….always deeper within yourself, to the sacred gift, the Inner Goddess.

Hava'iki

My feeling is that we are 'warriors' of consciousness and spirit being activated all over the world, and for me in the islands of Polynesia, from *Aotearoa*, land of the first light, and the first revelation of the prophecy of no-more-secrets, to ancient *Hava'iki*.

Within Your Cells

We hear news of 'new humans' in parts of the world being able to 'see' with various parts of their bodies. We can all open to this holographic way of seeing and knowing. Nothing is lost. It is coming from Within, from the very cells.

There are Always Solutions

The world, the biosphere, and human life is on the brink of extinction. This is mandatory evolution time. Yet there are already solutions on this planet even to life-threatening physical and emotional challenges, even to the most severe, chronic trauma, depression and PTSD. There are solutions to the life-threatening illnesses resulting from highly toxic GMOs, pesticides, heavy metal poisoning, geo-engineering chem trails, radiation, and more.

Anything and Everything Can Be Healed

In every cell of my being this is truth and this is reality that you can heal instantly. This is true for the indigenous peoples. When we believe beyond a shadow of a doubt that it is possible that anything can be healed, that changes everything.

Holo-Perception, a Simultaneous Perception

The consciousness I call Holo-perception is a bigger picture perception that all levels of reality, dimensions and paradigms exist simultaneously. When you face, embrace, encompass and hold them all simultaneously - that changes everything. I know from experience that having the conscious and the subconscious in congruency and coherence in the body and brain brings an authentic life of joy. It's the epitome of human fulfillment and accomplishment.

Consciousness, Holo - Perception with Aloha is the Key.

You then function as one with Aloha, Love, Light, Goddess, Nature, 'Universal Mind', or holographic mind, or indigenous mind, or God, or Source, as is your true calling. That's it, that's being here now, in 'zero point' energy.

A New Earth

We may then enjoy a society that rewards goodness instead of greed, and prioritizes people instead of profit.

I believe the ancients left within the oral traditions encoded messages, with specific application for our present times, which are indispensable for the planet's survival – and creation of a new civilization, a new earth - at this time. That is the secret of the inner experience and teachings of Aloha, which call to be spread far and wide for healing our planet in crisis.

One in The Goddess: the Power of Aloha in Sound and Music

*Goddess Revered in Hawaii *Aloha Sound Current *What Goddess Means to Me - "It was worth it, wasn't it?" *The Language of the Soul *The Love You Already Are*

"The Goddess in her archetype as the Divine Mother embodies all that exists in the manifest creation. She is intimately known and yet strange like nature, lovingly tender and yet cruel like fate, joyous and untiring giver of life, and mute implacable portal that closes upon the dead."

-- Jung

"Do you want to be part of the New Civilization?"

-- Antion

"When mankind accepts The Goddess there'll be Love, Light and Peace"

– *Jai Ma,* composed by Antion

Okay, I just have to add this additional chapter. I can't end this book without talking about the sound current of Aloha, the Goddess, the music, and Antion's CD, because it's so much what has led, guided, protected and inspired my journey.

My experience is that the sound current of the CD "One in The Goddess" is the sound current of *malama,* caring for, acknowledging and honoring Nature, sacred Heart, sacred Body, and sacred Earth.

It is the sound current of Aloha, of mahalo, of pono, of kuleana, of ohana. You realize that it is not about what you know but what you live.

Beyond but including the Love that you do, give, feel, express, create, make, long for, and talk about, the music engenders the feeling of already having it all...being the Love you already are.

The more you hear it the more you come into your own inner knowing of the sacredness of your embodiment. It heals original separation.

This is one of my many personal experiences of the Goddess:

One day, while driving along, I'm mourning a financial loss. I'm making the half hour drive south from Kilauea to Kapa'a, crying, feeling really horrible inside, depressed, a total failure. I've just received news that one who owes me money has declared bankruptcy. I was relying on this investment money to set up a center in Hawaii and now it's gone.

Suddenly, going down the long hill past Moloa'a, I'm hearing a heavenly, soulful, entrancing, beautiful Hawaiian woman's voice singing. It's playing on the radio, filling the car with healing loving sound. Immediately I break down sobbing, initially wailing with grief and sorrow but then, increasingly coming into a state of what is, wow! an indescribable bliss! I'm being submerged and embraced in this wondrous feeling of incomparable joy, into and through my heart and soul.

A voice speaks inside my head, saying "It was worth it, wasn't it?" I know it's the Goddess, and I know she's expecting and waiting for my response... waves of Aloha bliss are engulfing me, washing away my mind's agony... I know I am being asked to acknowledge my choice, my power of choice...so I say, "Yes". Peace enfolds me.

Antion's CD - One in the Goddess –

What others are experiencing, in their own words:

"I have just been diagnosed with breast cancer and was completing the task of calling my loved ones to tell them of the battle that I will be taking. I was listening to my cable's "SoundScapes" music channel. With tears rolling down my cheeks, I heard a piece from an album from "Antion". I caught only part of the title of the piece and none of the album's, but hearing it, I closed my eyes and felt an overwhelming sense of peace..."

– B.C. California

"I JUST LOVE IT!!! it's sooo beautiful and I just have play it all day long... it's a treasure from the universe... I absolutely love it and I want to thank you for bringing forth such beautiful waves of harmony and deepness... it's a gift from Heaven... It gives

me the feeling that Heaven is right here on Earth...".- Gloria Excelsias, Los Angeles

"This music is ineluctably lovely! The voice, the harmonies, the obviously deep-felt spiritual heart that shines right on through every song, its beautifully melodic focus -- makes for an album that shimmers with the magical energies of the goddess universe." - Diane Sward Rapaport - *"How to make & sell your own Recording"*

"Truly magnificent. So exquisite, deep, real and true".
– Solara, visionary author of "Star Borne" & "11:11"

"Before I even heard it, as I received the CD into my hand, I starting experiencing intense 'chicken skin' or 'truth chills'. This lasted non-stop for 3 or 4 minutes!" Ahna, teacher of Transdance

"Wow!!!!! Thank you sooooo much for your beautiful CD!!! I tell you, we have been looking for beautiful, melodic Hawaiian music for years......this is just what we have been looking for!!! It brings joy to our hearts and it is perfect for our seminars!!!"
-- Trish and Doug Regan, www.dolphinspiritofhawaii.com Big Island

"Antion's "One in the Goddess" CD is a powerful yet soothing journey into the Heart of the Goddess drawing from Hawaiian, East Indian and American traditions. It is created with an artistry that is profoundly beautiful, deeply dimensional and hauntingly touching. Remarkable in its clarity and intensity, this spiritually healing and uplifting album has that quality of immaculate presence that you know comes from years of spiritual discipline and devotion".– David Kapralik, Manager of Musical Artists

"I realized that I may have listened to it close to 1000 times. I simply never get tired of it!!! So I practice yoga while I remember "why I've come to earth...to love, serve, and remember." -- Nancy, WA

"I purchased your "One in the Goddess" CD at CSL, and am moved in some deep place by the power and resonance of your voice. I listened to it for hours on a solo driving trip between Seattle and Banff, Alberta, Canada..." – Carol, NY

"*I never heard of you before, but somehow ended up on a website while surfing that played bits of your new Goddess CD. I immediately ordered it. I want to let you know that although I have never heard music that felt like this before, your music touches my soul*". - - Janet, CA

"*I wore it out and need more, love it!*" -- Wally "Famous" Amos, HI

"*I love it! It is wonderful!*"- --Frank Kawaikapuokalani Hewitt, Kumu Hula, healer Kahuna, singer songwriter, chanter, and source of some of the songs and chants on Antion's CDs HI

"*I immediately fell in love with it! Thank you for giving us the privilege of carrying your CDs. I find deep peace and love shining through your music. Your spirit and love is beautiful to see.*" --- Linda Lester, President, www.Hawaiianmusicstore.com

"*Every single person who receives a session with the music has had an awesome experience and fallen in love with both my work and the music!*"-- Saharah Dyson, Retreat Center Director HI

"*Wore it out twice, can't live without it!*" -- Kathy, NY

"*Antion has produced a masterpiece that will touch you deeply. "One in The Goddess" is Antion's gift of Love and Joy to us all. 'Magnificent Treasure' is how I am best able to describe this beautiful offering. He has held nothing back and it is so very plain to see/hear/feel that this is a testament to his profound musical mastery. The performances are impeccably conceived and resplendent with lush vocal harmonies, masterful instrumentals, and of course, Antion's beautiful singing. It might be nice to put a label like, "The Voice of Kaua'i", on this CD, but Antion has shown, with this offering, that he is truly a "world class" talent.*"- - Robert Pearson, EMF Balancing, Switzerland

That's it. To me Aloha sound current is The Goddess, the frequency and vibration and sound and music of God, Goddess, Aloha, and Hawai'i. It's the sound current of the CD and of this book.

I was born with a vision

And a mission

To find, feel, and practice Love on Planet Earth

Thereby helping increase the Power of Love

It is Love that Engenders the extraordinary and miraculous

It's Love that Generates natural ageless living

It's Love that Gives birth to miracle healing

It's Love that Enables invincible super health

It is Love that Changes Everything

Epilogue

"But the makers of legend have seldom rested content to regard the world's great heroes as mere human beings who broke past the horizons that limited their fellows and returned such boons as any man with equal faith and courage might have found.... The hero comes back from this mysterious adventure with the power to bestow boons on his fellow man."

-- Joseph Campbell

The benefits of a hero's journey are for you to claim.

We all have our authentic voice and expression that calls to be recognized. When you look at your life in terms of the hero's journey you recognize that life's painful experiences are your true credentials. They are your qualifications, not to be given by another! but yours to claim. You can then receive the 'rewards' or gifts from those losses.

There's only the one caveat: you must claim your own authority to do so!

That is the meaning of the word 'responsibility' according to the Encarta dictionary. It's not about taking the blame for something, nor is it only about "responding, the ability to respond to", no, it really means claiming your authority, your self-sovereignty. It is your privilege and power to claim responsibility for yourself.

No one can do it for you, nor is meant to.

So, for example, my challenges and struggles blessed me with the following gifts to claim as benefits and credentials:

• Surviving radical transformation six times

• Reinventing myself five times

• Four decades of daily meditation (millions of hours)

• 17 years white-robed ashram living

• Daily disciplined self-care, self-healing practices

• Over 41 years TV free, meat-free vegetarian, alcohol free, drug free, caffeine free, and (mostly) processed-white-sugar free - & addiction-to-shopping free!

• Five years of outdoor close-to-nature minimalist eco-living in yurt

• Receiving and developing my own unique work

• Presenting thousands of healing sessions incorporating 33 healing modalities, plus trainings worldwide

• Developing a conviction that what I have done and can do, anyone can do, you too!

• Ability to transmit this consciousness

• Maintaining wonderful health in older years

• Sustaining personal lasting increasing love with partner (41 years)

• The joy of being - what I love to be! - a passionate proponent of joyous co-creative consciousness...

My forthcoming books Volumes 2 and 3, continue the interweaving of my stories into a deeper definition and transmission of Holo-Perception consciousness and how it works for your benefit.

With Holo-Perception you may:

• Know the (holographic) truth that we are all connected, and being "in this together" we can do anything

• Activate the unused 90% of your brain and bring all parts into congruency

• Increase conscious awareness – currently at only about 5% in most of humanity - of the subconscious which actually runs your life

• Listen inside to your body. Commune with your cells and organs to know a new relationship with your body

• Hear your inner voice and guidance and take it as for real, so you may act upon it

• Self-heal both your physical and emotional challenges, even the most severe, chronic trauma, depression and PTSD, even life-threatening illnesses. Even the highly toxic effects of GMOs, pesticides, heavy metal poisoning, geo-engineering, chemtrails and radiation

•Reclaim energy from inner and outer negativity (fear, pain, anger, grief, confusion) and use it like an alchemist for your fulfillment

• Maintain your body 5 -15 years younger than your chronological age

• Make friends with death and dying

• Supercharge your ability to heal self and others.

• Know that the devastation wrought by the ongoing economic turmoil is the very gift that can change your life for the better

• Calmly preside unscathed over the inevitable crises and catastrophes of the times knowing - "We are in the biggest transformation of consciousness the world has ever seen."- Satya Sai Baba

• Be able to measure, calibrate, discern and choose for yourself - what really matters!

• Rejoice together in co-creation, with lots of healthy fun!

We are the Voices of Sacred Earth

Rising up and speaking out

We are the people of peace, the Waitaha

We are the people of love, the Cathars

We were the persecuted and martyred innocents of history

We were the matriarchs, priestesses, goddesses

The maligned feminine in both men and women

We are the truth speakers, the star elders

We are the Waka of the Stars, heroes now

Back to reclaim our peoples,

Our families, our children, our lands

To heal, feel, give and forgive

We, the peoples of Love

Did not come back for nothing

We are here to give life and purpose

Simplicity, joy and divinity in action

We are the Voices of Sacred Earth

Joyously singing as One

Closing Circle at Kawai Purapura, New Zealand - 2013

"Come on people now...

Smile on your brother, everybody get together

Try to love one another right now".

--Dino Valenti, *"Get Together"*

People, friends, I love you, a hui hou, (see you soon!)

From Stardom to Wisdom

Acknowledgements

To you the reader, thank you for reading this book, and bless you on your own "Hero's journey!"

I would love to give thanks and name all my support but that would make a book in itself. So briefly:

Great mahalo to my ever present "unseen friends and helpers".

Mahalo to my beloved husband of over 40 years for your undying love, support and your extraordinarily transformational God-Goddess-inspired music.

Most of all, great mahalo to my ancestors and teachers. Knowing we as descendants and students stand on the shoulders of those who came before, I have a huge gratitude for you all.

Thank you worldwide supportive friends, students and clients.

Mahalo my Kaua'i friends for your support during the writing: Joan Levy, Ken and Jan Bernard, Penny Prior, Craig Maas, Barbara Curl, Vigil Alkana, Richheart Wonder, Roxanne McDougal, Ken and Chris Carlson, Laura Michelle, Amy, Susan and many more.

To my dearest friend, Teresa Schoch, thank you for believing in me. Mahalo, my Hawaiian shaman friend the late Nahi Guzman, for recognizing that which was pono in my work in the Hawaiian way, and mahalo especially Michael Fleck, for your writing support over the years, and to Lauren Orlina, for your editing and enthusiasm.

For writing support , thank you Gay Hendricks, Steve Manning, Transformational Authors, and friends Eve Hogan, Kamala Rose, Oscar Martinez, Dennis Starkovich, Dena Sax, Facebook supporters, - and many more. Donna Kozik of Write a Book in a Weekend, I could never have done it without you; healing and baby-birthing are easier than book-birthing. I can't wait to show up on your website - joining the thousands of your authors - with book in hand whooping wildly "Yippee! What a miracle!"

About the Author

Elandra Kirsten Meredith was born in Denmark and raised in New Zealand. As a London model and actress she experienced a spiritual epiphany and abandoned her celebrity lifestyle in favor of yoga teaching and ashram eco-living.

After several decades as director of a Yoga Center, she experienced a miraculous healing which catalyzed her true vocation as a transformational healer and teacher.

Elandra, CMT, LMT, BA, is known worldwide as a 'medical intuitive' miracle healer, consciousness catalyst, researcher, author, and teacher with over thirty years' experience as professional multimodality practitioner in five Healing Centers, practicing 33 healing modalities.

She is founder, director and international teacher trainer of:

Lomi Chi Holographic Healing

Online Elandra Health Healing Program

Living Love Kundalini Yoga for the New Earth®

Sacred Sites and Sounds Journeys®

WOW! Walking Our Wisdom®

WOW! Wildly Organic Women®

Elandra's Website: www.healthhealing.org

www.kundaliniyogainternational.wordpress.com

News and TV interview - story-of-love-yoga-and-vampires/ TV3NZ

Sessions & Trainings Background:

http://healthhealing.org/aboutus/lomichi.htm

Online Program - http://healthhealing.org/buy-now/

Testimonials: http://healthhealing.org/aboutus/

healingbodywork.htm Facebook, LinkedIn, Twitter, and Skype –

Elandra dot Meredith

About Elandra and Antion

Elandra & Antion Love Co-creating

Elandra with her husband of 41 years - 60s rock star turned yoga teacher, transformational sacred guitarist, singer and chanter - co-create international workshops and retreats in Kundalini Yoga for the New Earth®, Naad Yoga-Sacred Voice®, 7 Secrets of Lasting Happiness in Relationship, Transformational Yoga for Men in the Age of the Divine Feminine and more.

Antion's website is www.antionmusic.com

They are based in Auckland New Zealand, and Hawaii USA, while travelling and teaching internationally. In New Zealand their work is hosted yearly at two retreat centers: www.kawaipurapura.co.nz www.Prana.co.nz

Antion & Elandra's Vision

Their sessions, music, concerts, workshops, books, CDs are focused on raising consciousness with the use of sacred sound and voice, promoting the core oneness of all people and denominations, respect for women and the Divine Feminine, and the healing of the Earth and her peoples.

More about their background

Rich in yoga lifestyle discipline for 41 years, Yoga teachers/ directors of Ashram Yoga centers for 20 years, integrating 20 years of earth-centered

Taoist and Hawaiian Healing spirituality, they are free spirited international leaders, healers, specializing in empowering consciousness for the joyful evolution of humanity.

As movie star and rock star they left behind the 60s world of celebrity fame and fortune to embrace authentic spiritual values in ashram yoga community. Antion was the first Kundalini Yoga teacher in Europe, and together they were directors of the San Diego California Kundalini Yoga Centre and Ashram from 1977 to 1991.

After 21 years in California they transitioned to Kaua'i, Hawai'i for 17 years of immersion in Aloha, miracle healing, shamanism, chant, ageless wisdom and 'indigenous mind' consciousness. Together they are celebrants, see http://healthhealing.org/aboutus/weddings.htm, and love to lead Sacred Sites and Sounds Journeys, see www.healthhealing.org http://healthhealing.org/aboutus/sacredsites.htm

Celebrating Ageless Living and Loving for over 40 Years

Ant-El Productions – Books, CDs – How to Order

Yoga for Health and Healing – Elandra Kirsten Meredith with Alice Clagett is available through http://2u3d.com/yoga/yhh_reviews.htm - see 5 star reviews. All her yoga books co-created with Alice Clagett include:

Survival Kit: Meditations and Exercises for Stress and Pressure of the Times, and Relax and Rejoice: a Marriage Manual

They may be ordered at http://2u3d.com/yoga/alice-and-elandra.htm

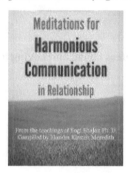

This updated eBook version of Harmonious Communication from the teachings of Yogi Bhajan, Ph.D., comes as valuable support in these times of great worldwide stress. These powerful meditations with specific breathing and the sounding of mantras have transformational power. They provide insight and support to singles seeking love and commitment, or for those already in relationship wanting strengthening, healing, change and transformation

Available in the Kindle Edition at http://www.amazon.com/Meditations-Harmonious-Communication-Relationship-Meredith-book/dp/B00CHGNOB2/ref=sr_1_4?ie=UTF8&qid=1385327017&sr=8-4&keywords=harmonious+communication

Antion's CD One in The Goddess - frequently repeat-ordered (due to being worn out from non-stop playing) is available at his web site: www.antionmusic.com

Antion's CD of Live Hawaiian Music; also available from his web site.

One in the Goddess and his other titles may also be purchased through http://www.invinciblemusic.com/mm5/merchant.mvc and CDBaby http://www.cdbaby.com/Search/YW50aW9u/0

See testimonials at http://healthhealing.org/music

See videos on YouTube "Antion Vikram Singh" Videos include Sikh Sacred
Kirtan, Hawaiian music with hula, yoga and more.
http://www.youtube.com/results?search_query=antion+vikram+singh&o
q=antion+vikram+singh&gs

Also on You Tube, see Antion as 'Vic Briggs' in videos of Eric Burdon &
the Animals

Elandra/Antion's work is for you if you are interested in:

Transformation, quantum Consciousness, super Consciousness, yoga,
miracle healing, ageless living, sound healing, sacred chant, eco-living,
multi-dimensional realities, Nature, hyper communication, sacred
relationship, ancient timeless wisdom, reinventing oneself, Hawaii, Aloha,
sacred activism and visions and practical strategies for a New Civilization
and a New Earth.

I love you and love to hear from you! elandra@healthhealing.org

Made in United States
Troutdale, OR
08/07/2024

21839014R00126